OPERATION NORTH POLE

OPERATION NORTH POLE

UNRAVELLING THE TRUTH BEHIND THE EXECUTION OF 50 **SOE AGENTS** IN THE SECOND WORLD WAR

STEPHEN WYNN

Pen & Sword
MILITARY

AN IMPRINT OF PEN & SWORD BOOKS LTD.
YORKSHIRE – PHILADELPHIA

First published in Great Britain in 2024 by
Pen & Sword Military
An imprint of
Pen & Sword Books Ltd
Yorkshire – Philadelphia

ISBN 978 1 39900 0 130

Typeset in INDIA by IMPEC eSolutions
Printed and bound in England by CPI Group (UK) Ltd., Croydon, CR0 4YY

Pen & Sword Books Limited incorporates the imprints of Archaeology, Atlas,
Aviation, Battleground, Digital, Discovery, Family History, Fiction, History,
Local, Local History, Maritime, Military, Military Classics, Politics, Select,
Transport, True Crime, After the Battle, Air World, Claymore Press, Frontline
Publishing, Leo Cooper, Remember When, Seaforth Publishing, The Praetorian
Press, Wharncliffe Books, Wharncliffe Local History, Wharncliffe Transport,
Wharncliffe True Crime and White Owl.

For a complete list of Pen & Sword titles please contact

PEN & SWORD BOOKS LIMITED
47 Church Street, Barnsley, South Yorkshire, S70 2AS, England
E-mail: enquiries@pen-and-sword.co.uk
Website: www.pen-and-sword.co.uk

or

PEN AND SWORD BOOKS
1950 Lawrence Rd, Havertown, PA 19083, USA
E-mail: uspen-and-sword@casematepublishers.com
Website: www.penandswordbooks.com

During the writing of this book my mother-in-law sadly passed away. She was a loving mother to my wife Tanya, and wife to her late husband Johnny. She loved animals, especially dogs, which she had all her life, and is sorely missed by all who knew her.

Romaine Grace Wilkinson,
14 March 1938 – 19 December 2022

Contents

Introduction

In Dutch it is referred to as *Englandspiel* (England Game), in English Operation North Pole, and in German *Unternehmen Nordpol* (Operation North Pole), but no matter which title one chooses to use, the outcome was the same; a resoundingly successful counterintelligence operation for the Abwehr, Germany's military intelligence agency.

Operation North Pole was a catastrophic failure for the Special Operations Executive (SOE) and the Dutch resistance movement, although it should not have been that way because the eventual outcome was avoidable. What it became, however, was the best example of how *not* to conduct clandestine operations.

Soon after becoming Prime Minister, Winston Churchill came up with the idea of creating a select group of individuals who would serve behind enemy lines in German-occupied countries and undertake acts of irregular warfare such as sabotage and subversion. Their instructions were to 'set Europe ablaze'.

The Dutch resistance during the Second World War had more than enough volunteers, but what it really lacked to allow it to be a truly effective threat to the occupying German forces were weapons, explosives and wireless sets. The role of Section N within the SOE was created to deal specifically with such operations throughout the Netherlands. As a country the Netherlands possessed little in the way of woods and forests, where dedicated resistance fighters could hide out in relative safety. Nor were there many available areas for Allied aircraft to land, which meant detecting such landings much easier for the Germans to be able to control.

The other issue was that the Netherlands was occupied by forces of Nazi Germany, which made it extremely difficult for either members of the Dutch resistance or the SOE to hold up immediately before carrying out attacks on German troops or other designated military targets. The main issue for the Dutch resistance in the early part of the war was that they appeared to lack any kind of substantive or combined leadership; the groups which existed at that time did so independent of each other. It could be argued that from a security aspect this was a good thing, because if somebody betrayed other members of the group, the numbers lost would be lower than they otherwise would have been. On the other hand, the opportunity to make the resistance movement in the Netherlands a much stronger and effective organisation was much harder to achieve.

Operation North Pole officially lasted between 13 February 1942 and 1 April 1944. During this time a total of fifty-four SOE agents, mainly Dutch, were parachuted into the Netherlands and almost immediately captured by the Germans. Fifty of those were subsequently executed. Possibly more importantly than the agents themselves, however, were the wireless sets they brought with them, because once the Germans had obtained the cyphers used to operate them, the agents, in effect, became expendable. The Germans then used each of the agents' personal codes to make SOE bosses back in Britain continue to send more agents, weapons, radios and other supplies to the Netherlands. These agents, and all their equipment, were then subsequently captured by the Germans.

What is truly incredible about the story of Operation North Pole is that it managed to go on for as long as it did, without anyone on the British side apparently having any clue that it was taking place. Was that ignorance, incompetence, infamy or a combination of all three?

The story involves a number of people, but a lot of what is known about the SOE as an organisation comes from an individual who served with the unit as an intelligence officer, Michael Richard Daniell Foot, CBE, TD, who wrote a detailed book about the history of the SOE. He died on 18 February 2012, aged 92.

Although Lieutenant Colonel Hermann Giskes, head of the military intelligence department of the German military forces during the Second World War, and also the man in charge of the counterintelligence department of the Abwehr in the Netherlands between 1941 and 1944, not to mention the Abwehr as a whole, were unaware of it, the operation to drop SOE agents into the Netherlands was close to being ended by the British authorities, mainly because the RAF suspended all such flights to the Netherlands after May 1943. This came about because the RAF had noticed they were losing both aircraft and crew in far greater numbers than they would have expect for such flights.

A pattern had emerged which had not been recognised, or was simply ignored, by those in charge of running and directing SOE operations into the Netherlands. The RAF had noticed that not only had they not lost one of their aircraft on the approach to any of their landing areas or drop zones, they had never come under any kind of ground fire either. On a number of occasions, however, their aircraft were fired upon on the return flight to Britain, resulting in the loss of twelve of their aircraft and crews.

The SOE flights to the Netherlands were not stopped because those in England had worked out that their agent network had been compromised, but simply because the RAF had refused to sanction anymore flights and had withdrawn the use of their aircraft. When the Abwehr's commander in the Netherlands, Lieutenant Colonel Hermann Giskes, sent his taunting message to the SOE on 1 April 1944 complaining that there had been a noticeable lack of business sent to him by the British in recent times, it is more than likely he believed that they had finally worked out what had been happening with their agents, little knowing in reality it was all down to the RAF.

The full content of Giskes message was as follows:

To Messrs. Blunt, Bingham, and Successors, Ltd.
You are trying to make business in Netherlands without our assistance (Stop)
We think this rather unfair in view of our long and successful co-operation as your sole agents (Stop)
But never mind, whenever you will come to pay a visit to the Continent you may be assured that you will be received with the same care and result as all those who you sent us before (Stop)
So long, Hermann Giskes

It is sad that a lot of what took place could and should have been prevented by the authorities who were in charge of the British agents and the SOE, but for some inexplicable reason, what should have happened did not; a mistake which resulted in the deaths of fifty of the captured agents.

CHAPTER ONE

Why Did Operation North Pole Take Place?

An intriguing aspect about Operation North Pole is the question of why it took place. What was its purpose? What was it ultimately put in place to achieve, and why did it require so many agents?

The main purpose of the SOE in sending agents into the German-occupied Netherlands was to recruit Dutch civilians, train them, provide them with weapons, explosives, and radios, and then turn them into effective resistance groups nationwide so that they could fight the Germans from within. For this to work, all the groups, although independent of one another, needed their activities to be in keeping with what the Allies required, with a future invasion of German-occupied Europe as the ultimate goal.

An effective group would need to be able to carry out acts of sabotage, assassinations and subversion, whilst at the same time managing not to draw too much attention to themselves. At times it was a fine balancing act for these resistance groups, because the Germans were not against carrying out wanton acts of retaliation against the civilian population by means of violent reprisals, which usually resulted in innocent people being murdered. The more outrageous the act of sabotage carried out by the resistance was, the more civilians were killed as a result.

The planning for the eventual Allied invasion of the Normandy beaches in northern France gathered pace when the United States entered the war in December 1941, following the Japanese attack on Pearl Harbour. However, it began in earnest following the Washington Conference in December 1941 and January 1942, when both Britain and the United States agreed on a strategy of 'Europe first', before dealing with Japan.

An important part of the invasion plan was for resistance fighters to be able to support the amphibious landings by putting out of action or incapacitating enemy transport systems by blowing up bridges, railway lines, and roads, along with lines of communications. But such activities were not just carried out in France, but also in the surrounding lowland countries such as Belgium and the Netherlands, to ensure German reinforcements of both manpower and equipment could not be moved closer to the immediate area of the invasion landings.

The Allied command felt that although resistance fighters were well-intended, most had little if any military training or know-how. They needed proper military direction and leadership to ensure maximum effectiveness was derived from their actions. This is where agents from the SOE came in. Men and women who had the required skill sets to work with and lead these units, and who were prepared, willing and able to work behind enemy lines, whilst knowing full well that if they were captured by the Germans, their life expectancy would be short whilst their deaths would likely be brutal and involve torture.

Although Operation North Pole was a resounding victory for the German Abwehr, at the cost of the lives of at least fifty SOE agents, it could also be argued that other than a good public relations victory for the Germans, nothing was really achieved by either side. The Netherlands was never going to be the location for the D-Day landings; the number of German troops stationed there was never going to be increased that drastically because of the SOE's attempts at landing a number of its agents in the region. The objective may have been to raise the levels of Dutch resistance activity across the country and ensure that German troops would remain there and would not be sent to France, where the D-Day landings eventually took place.

CHAPTER TWO

The Special Operations Executive

The Special Operations Executive, more commonly referred to by the initials SOE, was an organisation officially formed on 22 July 1940. The man who had overall political responsibility for the newly formed division was Hugh Dalton, the Labour politician and Minister of Economic Warfare in the wartime government. Dalton had almost single handedly been responsible for the Labour Party's foreign policy throughout the 1930s and was a leading advocate of taking a tough stance against the rising threat of a Nazi-dominated Germany, one not necessarily shared by Neville Chamberlain, who during his term as British Prime Minister had preferred a policy of appeasement rather than disagreement or confrontation.

Dalton was a clever man, educated at both Eton, and King's College, Cambridge, and was an individual who fully immersed himself in student politics; his socialist views earned him the nickname of 'Comrade Hugh'.

Like Churchill, Dalton had served during the First World War as a lieutenant, initially with the Army Service Corps before transferring to the Royal Artillery. For his actions during the retreat from Caporetto on the Italian front on 24 October 1917, he was awarded the Italian military decoration the *Medaglia di Bronzo al Valor Militaire*, in recognition of his 'contempt for danger'; a similar attitude for many of those who served in the ranks of the SOE. He also saw active service in France. By the outbreak of the Second World War, he had been involved in politics for around fifteen years, and on 15 May 1940 he became the Minister of Economic Warfare; a position he held until 22 February 1942, when he was removed from his post. Two possible reasons for this decision were his use of SOE phone tapping equipment to listen in on the conversations of a number of his fellow politicians, or because some within the clandestine world of military intelligence were concerned with his socialist tendencies.

In simple terms, the SOE's main objective was to infiltrate countries occupied by Nazi Germany and other Axis powers, where they would engage in acts of irregular warfare such as sabotage and subversion, which would hopefully ensure that German forces had to remain on high alert. One of the ways SOE agents achieved this was to establish links with local resistance groups and supply them with weapons and other useful pieces of equipment delivered by RAF parachute drops.

This was an important aspect of Allied policy because Churchill was genuinely concerned that the longer countries were occupied by German forces, the more likelihood there was that the local civilian population would more readily collaborate with the occupiers.

The SOE had a number of different sections, each being responsible for a specific country. A total of some 13,000 individuals worked for the organisation, with nearly a quarter of these being women.

To deal specifically with their clandestine operations throughout the Netherlands, the SOE created what they called Section N, which, having come into existence on 20 December 1941, was initially based at the St. Ermins Hotel in Westminster, and afterwards at what was then known as the Metropole Hotel, near to Trafalgar Square.

During the war, Section N had four chiefs. The first of these was Major Richard Laming, who by the end of the war had become the Commercial Counsellor at the British Embassy to the Netherlands, which was located in south-west London. The other chiefs were Major Charles Blizzard, who was more commonly known by the nickname of 'Blunt'; Major Seymour Bingham, who had been Blizzard's deputy and who took over in March 1943; and Richard Iver Dobson, who took over in March 1944. The latter was commissioned as a 2nd Lieutenant on 18 April 1941 and originally worked for MI6.

As so many of the agents who were sent to the Netherlands did so whilst Major Bingham was in charge of Section N, it is almost inconceivable to think that there must have been those, both inside and outside of the organisation, who did not give some thought to the idea that he might have been working as either a German spy or a double agent.

The men in charge of Germany's military intelligence in the occupied Netherlands were Lieutenant Colonel Hermann Giskes of the Abwehr, and Joseph Schreider of the Sicherheitsdienst, or SD, which was the intelligence service of the SS. These two men proved to be more than formidable opponents and managed to sustain their operation of subterfuge for nearly two years, something which British military intelligence had not got anywhere near managing against the German Abwehr.

The detailed and intense training for prospective SOE agents came in four stages, beginning with an assessment of a prospective candidate's character. If a candidate failed this element of the process, that was it. There was no second chance or the opportunity to progress to the next stage. Because very little had been disclosed about what the SOE actually was, or what it did, security was not really an issue. For those who passed the selection, it was off to Scotland, but what they would be put through next was far from being a holiday. It was as rugged and taxing as the terrain they found themselves in. The course included physical training, weapons handling, unarmed combat, elementary demolitions, map reading, field craft and training in the use of radio communications.

For those who failed at this stage of proceedings, they were 'requested' to sign a non-disclosure agreement preventing them from talking about what they knew of the existence of the SOE.

The candidates who managed to survive the demands of the Scottish wilderness then faced a trip to Manchester. It was there that they underwent their parachute training, part of which was carried out in a large hanger at RAF Ringway. To pass this part of the training, students had to successfully carry out at least two jumps, one of which would be from an aircraft and other from a balloon platform. The reality was that operationally they would be dropped from extremely low heights, in the region of just 500 feet, which gave an agent around 20 seconds before they hit the ground and therefore left absolutely no room for error. If the jumps were carried out from above that height, there was a greater chance that the aircraft would be picked up by enemy radar operators, which might just result in the aircraft being shot down. The agents carried a shovel as part of their equipment so that they could quickly bury their parachute on landing. This was an extremely important aspect of their mission and was for their own safety; the longer the agents could remain undetected after making their landing, the better it was for them. Ensuring that their parachute was not discovered could literally mean the difference between life and death.

The final part of the candidate's training was held at Beaulieu in the New Forest, Hampshire, on Lord Montague's 7,000-acre country estate. Those who had made it this far were trained in the skills of breaking and entry, sabotage, forgery, and how to kill somebody quietly without them having the time or ability to call out. They were even taught how to live off the land. Only once candidates had successfully finished all elements of their training would they be considered for a live deployment behind enemy lines. The time period between an individual finishing their training and going live varied, but in most cases, it would only be a matter of weeks.

As the war years continued, the training methods for SOE candidates evolved as a greater understanding of the stresses that agents faced in the field became more apparent. More emphasis was placed on a student's psychological make up, how they dealt with stressful situations, and how they managed to carry out the tasks they were set whilst dealing with such stress. The new training methods were encapsulated into what became known as the Students' Assessment Board, which took place over a four-day period at Cranleigh, Surrey.

Students still had to attend a three-week course in Inverness-shire, Scotland, where what would be classed as the soldiering aspect of the training took place. This included training in the use of a number of different firearms, tactics, field craft, elementary Morse code, the planting of explosives and map reading. The course always started with a physically demanding route march over the rugged and unforgiving terrain of the local countryside. The conditions were exactly the same for both men and women alike and were certainly not for the feint hearted. Very few students were fortunate enough to get through it without sustaining cuts and bruises, and the odd broken bone or two were not uncommon occurrences.

Another element of the course focused on how to break into properties either by learning how to pick a lock or to make a copy of the key by taking an impression of it in a small slab of plasticine, which they would then carry with them, concealed in a matchbox.

The training was made as realistic as possible. This included students being taken to a nearby town or city and told to follow a particular individual, report on his movements, whether they spoke to anyone, what was said, and where they eventually ended up. The students had to think on their feet and be prepared for the person they were following to suddenly flag down a taxi, jump on a bus, catch a train, or stop at a café. They had to learn the art of not getting too close to draw attention to themselves, but to get close enough to hear what was being said if the person they were following stopped to talk to somebody or made a phone call. If, during the course of these tests, the students came to the notice of the police, they had in their possession a phone number they were to hand over so that their identity could be confirmed, and an explanation provided as to what they were engaged in. Not all students decided on taking this course of action; some chose to try to talk their way out of the situation because they understood that once they were actively deployed in the field, the reality was that there was nobody to telephone to come and help them. They would be on their own, and if they could not convince their captors of who they were and what they were doing, then they were in serious trouble.

Possibly one of the most important aspects of being an agent was having a cover story about who they were, where they had come from, and what they were doing in the place they were in at a given moment in time. Knowing this verbatim could literally mean the difference between life and death. The rule of thumb for an agent in the field was to keep it simple and make claims to locations, buildings, people and landmarks that they had some kind of knowledge of. If an agent's cover story was too wide in its descriptive detail, it could have fatal repercussions if not remembered and recounted correctly.

Disguises could also be extremely helpful. Something as simple as wearing a pair of glasses, a hat, having a moustache, a different hair parting, or speaking in a different accent or language could completely change an individual's outward appearance, and help the agent stay one step ahead of the local authorities who were always on the lookout for strangers. For members of the SOE, the lengths to which they could, or would, go to in certain circumstances even included the use of plastic surgery.

Possibly one of the most important aspects of the pre-deployment briefing agents would have was the meeting with the liaison officer, who would go through a final check list making sure they had all the items needed for their operation and to confirm with them the exact location where they would be dropped. The last thing the liaison officer would do was hand the agent two sets of pills. One was a number of Benzedrine tablets, which could be taken as and when needed to keep the agent awake, the other was a single capsule of cyanide, which when bitten down on would result in death in just a matter of seconds. For some this would be a much preferable option to having to undergo hours and hours of potentially extremely painful torture.

The liaison officer also had the task of collecting the agent from their accommodation and taking them to the RAF station, or other location from where their aircraft was due to take off from. Once the agent was on board, the liaison officer's job was over. Beside the agent the only other people on the aircraft were the pilot and maybe a co-pilot, although that was not always the case, and the dispatcher, the man responsible for readying the agent for his jump. As the aircraft neared the jump site, the pilot would make contact with the dispatcher. This would be his signal to open a door which was usually in the floor of the aircraft's fuselage. The agent would stand up, walk the short distance to the open doorway, and the dispatcher would connect his parachute to the overhead metal line that ran the length of the aircraft. The agent would then sit down, with his feet dangling in the aircraft's open doorway. The red light would come on indicating it was time for the agent to prepare themselves to jump. The light would change from red to green, and they would then slip through the opening and within a matter of seconds, their parachute would engage, yanking them upwards, before they descended slowly towards the ground. The agents had to concentrate, especially as they approached the ground, because if they landed too heavily, a broken ankle or leg would more than likely be the outcome.

If the Gestapo were not waiting for them then they could begin their operation and start putting into practice everything they had been taught in their training. Unfortunately, for those agents who were part of Operation North Pole, their involvement in war time operations ended in the moments soon after they had landed. If they had not been captured on landing, it is questionable how long any of them would have remained at large because they would not have been aware that many of the ID cards they had been provided with were of poor quality and easily distinguishable from a real one.

The first agent the SOE dispatched to the Netherlands was 21-year-old Dutchman Jan Willem van Driel. He had made his way to England via Sweden in the early months of the war; an act that would later see him awarded the Dutch Cross of Merit. After arriving in England, he was approached by MI6 and asked if he would be prepared to return to the Netherlands as one of their field agents. He agreed to do so without any hesitation.

He was dropped by boat, which allowed him to land on a beach on the west coast of the Netherlands, near to Oostvoorne, late in the evening of 17 August 1940, but his mission did not get off to the best of starts when he lost his transmitter in the process of coming ashore. Without it he had no way of contacting London to let them know that he had arrived safely. In essence, van Driel's mission was over before it had even started. He had been tasked with building up a shipping network of vessels that could be used to get agents and other required individuals safely across the North Sea to England, as and when the need was required.

Van Driel took the decision to remain in the Netherlands rather than try to return to England, and utilise his skills and knowledge for the benefit of the Dutch resistance by teaching its members the skills and knowledge he had been taught whilst training to be an SOE agent in Britain. He survived the war and remained in the Netherlands, where he died on 24 February 1980, four days shy of his fifty-eighth birthday.

Van Driel's mission caused somewhat of a rift between the SOE and their Dutch counterparts, the Centrale Inlichtingendienst, or Dutch Central Intelligence Service (CID) because the two organisations were supposed to liaise and cooperate with each other, and in the case of van Driel this certainly did not happen. The man in charge of Dutch intelligence had no knowledge of van Driel's deployment, nor did any of his men, thus highlighting the rift between the two organisations. If that was not enough, the two men in charge of each of the organisations, Major Richard Laming of the SOE and François van 't Sant of the CID, did not even speak to one another, let alone trust one another.

On 13 June 1941, two agents sent by MI6 and the Dutch CID were dropped at Vledder, a Dutch village in the province of Drenthe, in the northern most part of the Netherlands. There is a discussion to be had about whether or not either of these two men were agents who were actually involved in Operation North Pole. They were sent to the Netherlands after SOE agent Lodo van Hamel, who was dropped on 14 October 1940, and before Aart Hendrik Alblas, another SOE agent, but what is more significant is the amount of coded and decoded messages that were found on one of them when they were arrested, which was then subsequently deciphered by the Germans. This information was then used to help the Abwehr with conducting their clandestine efforts, which would eventually become known as Operation North Pole. With this in mind, the men's story holds a relevant place in what culminated in the capture and murder of so many Allied SOE and MI6 agents.

Meanwhile, Johan Jacob 'Hans' Zomer and Wiecher Bote Schrage were part of what was known as Operation Zebra. Zomer was born on 6 November 1920 in Probolinggo, Java, in what was then the Dutch East Indies, where his father was posted with the Dutch Navy. Before the outbreak of the Second World War, and having returned to the Netherlands, Zomer studied at the Wageningen Agricultural College, where he was a student of Tropical Forestry, but in 1939, after just one year at school, he left to enlist in the Dutch Navy, once again becoming a student, but this time at the Dutch naval college in Den Helder.

With the German occupation of the Netherlands, many young Dutchmen wanted to carry on the fight, but to do this they had no choice but to try to make their way across the North Sea to England. On 14 May 1940, just three days before German forces completed their occupation of the Netherlands, Zomer and twenty-six other members of the Dutch Navy left the Netherlands on board HNMS *Medusa*, a Hydra class Minelayer, which had first been commissioned way back in December 1911.

Zomer was recruited by MI6 in early 1941, when he was just 20 years of age, and just a matter of months before he was parachuted back into the Netherlands to help build up a resistance movement in the area. During his training he used the name of A. Spencer. Once on active service he also used the aliases of Piet Smid, Piet Smit, Wim van Zetten, and Johannes Jacobus Smit, and his code name was 'Zebra 1'.

Zomer and Schrage took off from Newmarket's Rowley Mile racecourse just before 01:00 on 13 June 1941 in an Armstrong Whitworth Whitley, a twin-engine medium bomber aircraft. The pilot's name was Flight Sergeant John Austin, and he steadied his aircraft as he arrived in the skies above Vledder at 03:28. The bomb doors of the aircraft opened, and at a height of just 2,000 feet, Zomer and Schrage jumped. The aircraft was so low that the pilot and his crew actually saw the two men land in the middle of a field, but thankfully for them, there was no German reception committee waiting. The first thing they did was to hide their parachutes and equipment they had landed with, which gave the men time to fully take in their surroundings, try and make contact with some friendly locals, whilst at the same time making sure that the area was not inundated with German soldiers.

Zomer was captured by the German security police on 31 August 1941 whilst at the Sickenga family home in Bilthoven, a Dutch village in the province of Utrecht, as he was in the process of transmitting a message to London with information about an airfield used by the German Luftwaffe. The information had been provided by the Sickenga's son, Japp, who had also been a student at the Wageningen Agricultural College. When he was arrested, Zomer had in his possession a large number of messages, some of which were coded, but fortunately for the Germans, some of them were also uncoded and one of their own experts, Sergeant Ernst May, was able to decipher them.

Both Zomer and Sickenga were taken to the prison at Scheveningen to be interrogated. It was some eight months before the two men were put on trial at a Jesuit monastery in Maastricht. They were both found guilty of spying and sentenced to death, by which time Zomer was just 21. Late on the evening of 10 May 1942, along with more than twenty other young Dutchmen, he was transferred to the Sachsenhausen concentration camp, on the outskirts of Berlin, where he was executed by firing squad the following morning.

Whilst Zomer's job had been that of the radio operator, responsible for transmitting any messages which needed sending to London, Schrage's part in the operation was to gather the information for Zomer to send. Schrage, who 24 years of age and who had the code name of 'Visser', was fortunate that when the German soldiers discovered Zomer's exact location, he was not in the area and so managed to stay at large. The problem he now faced, however, was that no matter how much information he uncovered, without Zomer he had no way of transmitting it back to Britain, which in essence meant there was no point in him remaining in the Netherlands, as all he was doing was putting his own life at risk.

On the evening of 13 November 1941, less than three months after Zomer had been captured, and some six months before he was executed, Schrage and another stranded agent, Cornelis Sporre, who had been dropped into the Netherlands on 7 September 1941, set off from the Dutch village of Peeten in North Holland in a small boat. Although the weather was sufficiently calm for them to begin their journey, neither man was ever seen again.

Fortunately for the Allied nations, in the early years of the war, the effectiveness of German counterintelligence had not been as effective as it could have been, mainly due to professional differences between the Wehrmacht and the Secret Police. This was similar, in a way, to the relationship which the British Broadcasting Company (BBC) experienced with a number of British government secret service departments, with each having slightly different agendas. The point here is one of trust, regardless of whether the organisation was a state broadcasting service, the German secret police, an army unit or a government.

The BBC's European Service had been sending coded messages to Allied agents and local resistance pockets in German-occupied countries since the beginning of the war.

The other issue this raised was who was in overall charge, and who was responsible for deciding the level of importance given to any intercepted messages, and what, if anything, should be done about them. Continuity was of particular importance when it came to determining if a message sent from an occupied country was from an Allied agent or if it had come from Germany's Abwehr counterintelligence operative.

It was clear that for counterintelligence to be as effective as possible, it needed to be under the control of just one organisation. By way of example, the BBC, who during the Second World War continued to transmit its special language service and foreign language news bulletins via its European Service, had to come to an agreement with the 'Free French' and other governments who were in exile in London, as well as the Secret Intelligence Service (SIS), which was MI6, and the newly formed SOE, who understandably all had their own individual agendas. The need for such an agreement was possibly best highlighted with the desire by the Free French government who wanted to direct their agents' resistance operations in France, which was not necessarily the same as what British counterintelligence wanted them to do.

To ensure there was a singular and co-ordinated manner of the sending and receiving of messages to and from France, a document was drawn up entitled 'Handling of BBC Messages for the Fighting French', which covered operational messages and other SOE and SIS messages. The following is one of the paragraphs included in the document, which specifically refers to SOE and SIS messages:

These are likely to consist of messages requested by the Fighting French agent abroad, to establish confidence, etc., or they may emanate from this country in order to acknowledge the safe arrival of persons or documents. They may also consist of messages previously agreed with agents to indicate the departure of persons abroad that they are in danger and should take the necessary steps to protect themselves.

CHAPTER THREE

Leo Marks – SOE Bletchley Park

Who was Leo Marks? His real name was actually Leopold Samuel Marks, born into a devout Jewish family in London on 24 September 1920. His father, Benjamin Marks, was a co-owner of Marks & Co, an antiquarian book shop at 84 Charing Cross Road. It was to a large degree due to his father that Leo became interested in codebreaking and cryptography.

In January 1942, Marks, like a lot of young men of his age, was conscripted into the British Army, where due to the influence of one of his godfathers, who was a police officer in Special Branch, he became a cryptographer; a skill set which he had in abundance. His ability in the subject was obvious for his instructors to see, and unlike most of his contemporaries, who after completing their initial training were sent to hone their skills at Bletchley Park in Buckinghamshire, home of the main British code breaking centre, Marks was sent to work at Baker Street in Westminster, home to newly formed Special Operations Executive.

Marks proved his worth on his very first day of work when he was given a code to decipher and although it took him nearly all day to break (a task he had been expected to complete in less than half an hour) the reason it had taken him so long was because he had not been given the cipher key to begin the process with. Despite this, he still managed to break the code, which had been considered by his instructors to be unbreakable. This was an excellent example of what Marks saw as the organisation's somewhat laid-back attitude, and occasional lack of professional application. Not a trait he expected to encounter in the field of counterintelligence, where such a blasé approach could result in a man's untimely, and unnecessary death.

Marks knew one of the main factors that could mean the difference between life and death for agents in the field was the amount of time it took them to send a message. The longer they were 'online', the more chance their exact location would be discovered by the Germans. As was usual for these agents, their work meant they were constantly under a great deal of stress and pressure which could lead to mistakes when they were sending their encoded messages. When this happened, the usual procedure was for the operative at the home station in London to tell the agent to resend the message. Unintentionally, this placed the agent in extreme danger as it meant their position was more likely to be compromised and discovered by the German signal tracers, as the agents had to remain online a lot longer.

When an agent had to send a message, they did so in Morse code. The wireless sets used to send and receive messages by active agents operating behind enemy lines were big and cumbersome, and regardless of where an agent was when they sent or received their messages, the set required an external aerial which placed them in even more danger. If spotted by the Germans or a local informer, it would more than likely result in the agent's capture, detention, torture and death.

Marks was so good at his job that not only did he identify these inherent risks, but he also came up with a solution. Whilst working at Grendon Hall in Buckinghamshire, which was the SOE's Station 53a, he devised a process which allowed him and a hand-picked team of cryptologists to be able to analyse partially sent messages, or ones that appeared somewhat garbled, from agents operating behind enemy lines in occupied Europe and work out the correct meaning of the message. This system negated the need for the cryptologists, who were sitting comfortably in their nice, warm, cosy offices back in Britain, to have to ask the agents to resend their message. On most occasions, this came about as a direct result of Gestapo signal tracers tracking the agents' transmissions.

Having looked closely at the way in which the SOE communicated with its agents operating behind enemy lines throughout occupied

Europe, Marks was quick to replace the organisation's existing cyphers with new ones. Somewhat unbelievably, the SOE agents had been using well-known British poems and passages from classic works of English literature as the cyphers for encoding their messages. This meant that once it was known which particular poem the agent had used, it would be a relatively straight forward process for German cryptologists to decode a captured agent's messages.

The solution Marks came up with was actually quite simple. He continued to use poems as the cyphers to agents' messages, but changed them so that they were original ones, many of which he had written himself.

It was a remarkable achievement for Marks to be in charge of the SOE's codes and cypher section at just 22 years of age. He was also the first person to realise that there was a potential problem with the connections. He became so convinced he was right, he wrote a memorandum about what he felt, but his protestations fell on deaf ears when brought to the attention of the SOE's senior officers.

Brigadier, later Sir, Colin Gubbins, the overall head of SOE between 1943 and 1946, summoned Marks to explain himself and what he had written in his memorandum.

'What did you tell Colonel Tiltman about the Dutch situation?' Gubbins asked Marks.

'Nothing, sir. I was instructed not to discuss the country sections.'

'And you always obey your instructions?'

'No, sir. But in this instance, I did.'

(John Hessell Tiltman was a leading British figure in the field of cryptography, who during the Second World War worked at Bletchley Park where he was considered one of the finest cryptanalysts on non-machine systems.)

The response Marks repeatedly received concerning his worries about what was happening to the SOE agents in the Netherlands was not quite what he expected. Rather than show concern or be prepared to consider that his warnings might have some substance, his superiors, who in the main were born out of an old school British university education, wanted concrete proof. It was as if they did not want to believe that what he was suggesting had any foundation.

Marks' argument was that despite the extremely difficult circumstances these agents found themselves in, not a single Dutch agent had been so stressed out that they subsequently made a mistake when it came to sending their messages. He had also sent a dummy message to the Netherlands and signed it with the letters HH, a common German sign off at the time, meaning Heil Hitler.

By the end of the war, Marks had become the SOE's chief cryptographer and later in life published a book entitled *Between Silk and Cyanide: A Codebreaker's Story 1941-1945* about his wartime role in working with the SOE. He had actually written the manuscript for the book in the early 1980s, but was not given official approval for its publication from the British government until 1998. After the war he returned to civilian life where he earned a living writing scripts for theatre productions and films. Marks died from cancer on 15 January 2001.

CHAPTER FOUR

Lodo van Hamel and the Start of Operation North Pole

Operation North Pole 'officially' began with the arrest of Dutch secret agent Lodo van Hamel on 14 October 1940, but his part in the story actually began several weeks earlier.

Lodewijk Anne Rinse Jetze van Hamel, commonly referred to as Lodo van Hamel, was an experienced officer in the Royal Dutch Navy who had been commissioned as a Lieutenant 3rd class in August 1935. He was involved in the evacuation of Prince Bernhard and Princess Juliana, members of the Dutch Royal family, to Britain by ship on 12 May 1940. Not the type of individual to sit around and wait for things to happen, van Hamel made his way back across the English Channel to assist in the Allied evacuations from Dunkirk as the commander of the Dutch motor sloop *M74*. After the rescue of the remaining men of the British Expeditionary Force and other Allied soldiers was complete, the Dutch Navy was asked to provide a volunteer to return to the Netherlands, establish what life was like for the Dutch civilian population under German occupation, set up a radio connection with London, and link up with local resistance fighters who were more than capable of continuing the work he had begun.

The need for such a volunteer had arisen out of a request made from François van 't Saint, who at the time was head of the Dutch intelligence service. It was van Hamel who immediately volunteered for the mission.

Despite it being the Dutch Navy who were asked to provide a volunteer, the agent in question would not cross the Channel by sea, but rather be dropped by parachute. This was interesting as van Hamel had never had the need, or desire for that matter, to undergo a parachute jump. So, before he could return to his homeland, he first had to undergo a crash course at the RAF's newly established No. 1 Parachute Training School, at Ringway, near Manchester, under the command of Squadron Leader Louis Strange.

After carrying out a number of training drops in a specially adapted hanger at Ringway, one of which was during the hours of darkness, van Hamel was deemed ready to undertake his mission. Without any further ado, a Whitley Mk III bomber aircraft set off for North Weald airport in Essex. The aircraft usually had a five-man crew but for van Hamel's mission to the Netherlands, this was cut to three, with the wireless operator and rear gunner being omitted. The crew consisted of the pilot Flight Lieutenant Earl Bateman Fielden, co-pilot Squadron Leader Louis Strange, DSO, MC, DFC*, and Flight Lieutenant Marsh as the navigator, whilst an addition to the crew was Squadron Leader Donald Ross Shore, AFC, who was the 'despatcher'; the man who would assist van Hamel leaving the aircraft when they had arrived at their destination.

Late on the evening of Friday, 23 August 1940, the Whitley aircraft took off from North Weald airfield and headed across the North Sea towards its destination of Sassenheim, close to the west coast of the Netherlands, and some 5 miles north-east of Leiden. The weather forecast had indicated that the operation was good to go, but this turned out not to be the case. It was raining when they arrived, and the winds were gusting quite strongly. If van Hamel had been allowed to jump, there would have been absolutely no way of knowing where he would have eventually landed. The heavy winds could have resulted in him landing miles away from his intended destination. As if the weather conditions were not enough of a reason to abort the drop, just as the decision had been made to do so, the Whitley was caught in the powerful beam of a searchlight battery in the exact vicinity of where van Hamel was due to be dropped. Luckily, Fielden managed to escape the tracking of the searchlight, turn his Whitley around, and head out across the North

Sea without further issues, arriving back at North Weald at about 07:00 the following morning.

After a debrief about the aborted mission, and a few hours' sleep, van Hamel waited at North Weald to hear from the Air Ministry, whilst Fielden and the rest of the Whitley crew made their way back to RAF Ringway.

Having checked the expected weather conditions for the following days, the Air Ministry in London saw there would be an improvement on the evening of 26/27 August. The mission to drop van Hamel into the Netherlands behind enemy lines was back on.

This time, the Whitley crew included Sergeant David Bernard, who acted as the aircraft's wireless operator. Why it was deemed necessary to have a wireless operator on this flight and not on the initial one is unclear. Perhaps it was because if the mission had to be aborted once again, then the Air Ministry could be advised at the earliest opportunity?

This time, however, no problems were encountered on the mission, and Fielden took off from North Weald for a second time late in the evening of 26 August. Everything went according to plan, and with a marked improvement in the weather, van Halem was dropped near the Dutch town of Hillegom, in the region of South Holland, making him the first Allied secret agent dropped into the German-occupied Netherlands. Despite being his first actual parachute jump from an aircraft, van Hamel landed safely and met up with members of the local resistance movement, including Jo Allers, who had previously been a member of the Dutch intelligence service in The Hague, the location from where van Hamel transmitted his radio messages to London. Van Hamel had done an excellent job in just a matter of weeks, and with the assistance of the spy network he had set up, had sent a number of messages covering German troop movements, local airfields, the sighting of any German naval vessels spotted in or around the port of Rotterdam, or other information which he felt might have some military value.

With London happy, there was now a direct line of communication in place between themselves and the Netherlands, and the decision was made for van Hamel to return to London. The date for his extraction had been decided as 13 October 1940. A seaplane from the RAF's Dutch No. 320 Squadron, and flown by Heije Schaper, was allocated to pick him up from the large inland waterway in Tjeukemeer in the province of Friesland. Pretending to be a group of ornithologists studying the migration of birds in the area, van Hamel, Hans Hers, Jean Mesritz, Marion Smit, and Professor Lourens Baas Becking, who were all (except for Baas Becking) members of the Dutch resistance movement, spent all night in a small boat waiting for the arrival of the seaplane to arrive, but it never did. No reason was given for the seaplane's non-arrival, and van Hamel did not want to risk compromising his location by sending a radio message requesting an update. The five men tried again the following night, but although this time the seaplane did arrive, it was unable to land due to a low-lying fog.

Having realised they were not going to be picked up, and not wanting to spend a second night in their small boat, the men made their way back to shore. Although they had no way of knowing it, this would turn out to be a fateful decision for all of them.

Not long after coming ashore, van Hamel and his colleagues unfortunately bumped into two Dutch police officers, who understandably were somewhat surprised at discovering five men close to a beach in the early hours of the morning. This, quite understandably, made their cover story of being ornithologists harder for the two Dutch policemen to believe. Consequently, the five men were all detained and handed over to the Gestapo.

Unaware of the men's detention, Schaper returned to the area and landed on Lake Tjeuke on the evening of 15 October, but quickly escaped after being discovered and fired upon by German anti-aircraft guns. He managed to get airborne again, despite having his aircraft riddled with gunfire and two of his crew suffering injuries.

Whilst conducting a thorough search of the area where the men had been arrested, the Dutch police discovered a suitcase which they handed over to the Gestapo. Inside were incriminating documents revealing van Hamel to have been involved in acts of espionage. During his subsequent interrogation and torture, van Hamel did not reveal the name of a single person who had been involved with him in his activities. Amongst the paperwork found in his suitcase was the name 'Allers', a reference to the Dutch resistance fighter

Jo Allers, which led to the arrest of his entire family. When their house was searched, coded messages were discovered, but despite their best efforts, the Gestapo were unable to decrypt them. Van Hamel did eventually admit to being a British agent, but remarkably, his Gestapo interrogators refused to believe him. It was only when he showed them the location of his buried parachute that they realised he was telling the truth.

Van Hamel and the other prisoners were put on trial in April 1941 at the Supreme Court in The Hague. Hans Hers received a life sentence, Allers received ten years, Jean Mesritz was given three years, whilst Smit and Baas Becking were both acquitted. Van Hamel was not so fortunate as he received the death penalty, despite attempts by the Dutch government to try to arrange a prisoner exchange for a German agent who had been arrested in England. This attempt was thwarted by the intervention of Adolf Hitler, who refused to allow the exchange to take place; a decision which more than likely resulted in the execution of the German agent. Van Hamel was executed on 16 June 1941 in Bussummerheide and his body was cremated. He had just turned 26 years of age. As van Hamel was arrested in civilian clothing, the Germans were quite within their rights to execute him as a spy, something which van Hamel would have been aware of. Yet despite the inherent danger his own actions placed him in, he was still happy and willing to undertake his mission.

The suitcase which had been discovered soon after van Hamel's arrest was handed over to German military intelligence, the Abwehr, which led to the beginning of what became known as Operation North Pole. By the time it had come to an end, fifty agents of the SOE would be dead.

CHAPTER FIVE

Agents Captured During
Operation North Pole - 1941

The Nazis had four goals in mind for the Netherlands. The first of these was to transform the country into a national socialist state which could eventually become part of Nazi Germany. The second was to exploit the economic potential of Dutch industries, along with their labour force. The third goal was to purge the Netherlands of all Jews, and the fourth and final goal was to prevent any and all aid being provided to Germany's enemies through espionage, sabotage, and guerrilla activity.

If Allied agents could gain a foothold in the country's numerous underground movements, whilst remaining undetected, they could potentially help undermine Germany's iron grip over the Netherlands. But the men and women sent to help achieve this knew that the dangers they were placing themselves in could ultimately result in their own deaths.

While the actions of Lodo van Hamel have already been discussed, he was just one of a number of SOE and MI6 agents who were captured by the Germans during the time span of Operation North Pole. The following pages include the names of others who were involved, along with a brief resumé of each. The dates shown are the known dates they were dropped into the Netherlands, and the list also includes the names of MI6 agents who were dropped into the Netherlands during the lifespan of Operation North Pole, as over the years there has been some confusion as to the exact number of individuals who actually took part.

5 July 1941

Aart Hendrik Alblas, or to give him his wartime pseudonym, Klaas de Waard, was born in Middleharnis on 20 September 1918, the son of Cornelis and Maria Alblas. He enlisted in the Royal Dutch Navy, and on 3 September 1936, soon after his eighteenth birthday, he became a midshipman. The following year he attended the Maritime School in Rotterdam, after which time he became an apprentice coxswain. He went on to become one of the most highly decorated members of the Dutch resistance movement for his actions under the German occupation of his country. His story begins long before his eventual arrest.

It was during his time as an apprentice coxswain that he began patiently gathering information about the number of Chinese and Japanese ship locations, and movements between early 1940 and March 1941. Alblas, in company with his fellow resistance member Arnold M. Westerhout, escaped across the North Sea to England on the evening of 18/19 March 1941 in a motorboat, with both men dressed in stolen German uniforms. This was a daring feat as it meant a journey of more than 100 miles in unpredictable waters. The additional problem the men faced was convincing their British hosts that they were, in fact, members of the Dutch resistance and not German soldiers.

Dutch men and women who attempted to escape to England from the Netherlands in this way were known as *Engelandvaarder,* which literarily means 'English sailor'.

After convincing the British authorities of his identity and credentials, Alblas agreed to return to the Netherlands as an agent of Britain's MI6 and the Dutch CID, who had trained him in the use of wireless transmissions, and to gather intelligence on the known locations and movements of German forces. After having undergone some additional rudimentary training for his new role, he was dropped into the Netherlands by parachute on the evening of 5 July 1941, in the skies over Nieuweschans. Upon landing, he buried his radio equipment and then made his way to The Hague where, after a couple of introductions, he was put up by the Hueting family. Gerard Hueting was a prominent member of the Dutch resistance movement. Despite this obvious connection, Alblas informed Hueting that his name was Klaas de Waard.

It is unclear as to whether the Germans had been aware of Alblas' impending arrival as he was not actually a member of SOE. If they did know about it, they failed to locate him, as he remained at large for just over a year before eventually being captured on 16 July 1942. Gerard and Pum Hueting were arrested the same day but released just two weeks later. It would appear that the arrest of Alblas was the result of a betrayal, possibly by an individual who had infiltrated his circle of resistance friends and colleagues, but who was actually working for the Germans.

After Alblas was arrested, he was held at the prison camp in the old seminary at Haaren from 20 July 1942, where he remained until being transferred to another camp in Assen, before eventually arriving at Mauthausen concentration camp on 27 November 1943. Like all his colleagues, he was a very brave individual who not only understood the risks he was taking by becoming an agent, but also knew there was every chance that if he were captured, he would likely not survive the war.

Along with a number of other captured agents, most of whom were members of the SOE, Alblas was murdered by German guards at Mauthausen concentration camp between 6 and 7 September 1944. He was 25 years of age, and although not married, was engaged to his sweetheart, Pum Hueting, the sister of Gerard Heuting, and a nurse at the nearby Bronovo hospital. The couple had become close after Alblas moved into the family home.

In the years following the end of the war, Alblas was posthumously awarded the Military William Order, the Bronze Cross, the War Remembrance Cross, the Resistance Memorial Cross, and the King's/Queen's Commendation for Brave Conduct.

There is a suggestion that the reason for there being two dates, 6 and 7 September 1944, for the murders which took place at Mauthausen, is that some agents died whilst the others were murdered. At Mauthausen were a set of 186 steep, concrete steps, known as the Wiener Graben, infamously known as the 'Stairs of Death', which led up from the bottom of a quarry. It is suggested that on 6 September, a number of SOE agents held in the camp were forced to climb these steps whilst holding very large and heavy granite stones weighing more than 100 lbs. The men were made to repeatedly carry these stones up and down the steps until they died from the stress and strain of what they were being forced to do. If a prisoner stopped or dropped to their feet due to sheer exhaustion during the climb, they were routinely shot. There were those who also died as the result of being struck by one of the granite stones dropped by a collapsing or dying man in front of them.

The very next day, 7 September, those SOE agents who were still alive were instructed by their guards to do the same thing, but refused to do so and were shot dead by machine-gun fire.

1 October 1941

Johannes Hermanus Arnoldus Maria ter Laak was born in Tilburg on 23 May 1913. He was sent to the Netherlands by MI6/Dutch CID, landing in the area of Assen on 1 October 1941. As was in keeping with non-SOE agents who were sent to the Netherlands, he was eventually captured five months later on 13 February 1942.

Ter Laak is interesting in that he was not actually part of Operation North Pole, and his name is not included on the memorial at Mauthausen concentration camp, although he is shown as having died there on 7 September 1944.

7 November 1941

Hubertus Mattheus Gerardus 'Huub' Lauwers and Thijs Taconis were dropped into the Netherlands near Ommen on the evening of 7 November 1941, and although they were dropped at the same time, the two men did not stay together.

Lauwers was born on 19 July 1915 in Amsterdam and went on to become an intelligent young man, especially where languages were concerned. Besides his mother-tongue of Dutch, he was also fluent in English, French and German.

With Japanese forces becoming extremely active throughout Asia, including what was then known as the Dutch East Indies, Lauwers left his job as a journalist in Borneo, deciding he could best be of use elsewhere. He arrived in England on 23 October 1941, offered his services to the Dutch government in exile, and became a member of the Dutch section of the SOE. During his training he went by the name of Hubertus Mattheus Gerardus Lookman, and was given the code name of 'Ebenezer'.

Lauwers, who also used the alias of Lauwers Hubertus, sent his first back message to London on 3 January 1942, but was arrested just two months later on the evening of 6 March whilst in the act of sending wireless messages in Fahrenheitstraat in The Hague, near the home of Walter Teller, who was also arrested. After his arrest, Lauwers was initially detained at Scheveningen prison and coerced by the Germans into continuing with his transmissions to London, pretending he was still at large. Lieutenant Colonel Giskes, head of the counterintelligence department of the Abwehr in German occupied Holland between 1941 and 1944, and his team, already knew that Allied agents used what was known as a security check when they transmitted a message by Morse code, to prove they had not been compromised, but what they did not and could not possibly know, unless an agent freely gave it up, was what their individual security codes were. Lauwers had told Giskes and his men that his security check was simply to replace a stop with a dot each time he transmitted. The truth was that during his training he had been taught to mis-send every sixteenth letter if he had been compromised in any way.

He sent his first message for the Germans on 8 March 1942. As far as they were concerned he was being compliant and co-operative, but unbeknown to them, he had managed to mis-send every sixteenth letter of his message, which should have clearly informed those in London that he was not a free man, and was sending his messages under duress from the direct instruction of his German captors. In a dispatch sent on 28 March he even went as far as to include the letters CAU and GHT at the beginning and end of his message, but still the receivers in London did not appear to have fully understood what he was trying to tell them.

The obvious question is why did those in London not pick up on the fact that his messages included the agreed coded signal indicating that he was, in fact, a prisoner of the Germans? Maybe London saw this as an opportunity to convince the Germans they had been duped, and by going along with the attempted ruse they hoped they could convince them that the reason they were prepared to continue sending so many of their agents to the Netherlands was because that is where the eventual Allied invasion of occupied Europe would be. There must have been a time during the eighteen months that North Pole was operational that Giskes and his colleagues at German counterespionage, believing they had duped the British authorities, wondered why so many Allied agents were being sent over.

If London did, in fact, ignore Lauwers' attempts at informing them he had been arrested, it was a decision which ultimately cost the lives of some fifty Dutch wartime agents. Unfortunately, it is now highly unlikely that the truth of the matter will ever fully come to light.

Lauwers was liberated by Russian forces from the Rathenow concentration camp, in Brandenburg, on 26 April 1945, having previously been held at the prison camp at Rawicz, in Silesia.

There is the question of why he was not sent to Mauthausen along with the other captured British agents. Was it a favour by Giskes for the assistance he believed Lauwers had provided to the German war effort?

The website www.englandspiel.eu contains a typed letter dated 25 March 1986, sent from France by Anthony James to Doctor A. Korthals-Altes in the Netherlands. In essence it appears that Mr James was one of those who was involved in the training of Lauwers as a radio operator for his work with the SOE. In the letter, Lauwers is referred to by the name of 'Loopy'. Despite regulations to the alternative, the two men's relationship appears to have crossed over from simply being student and instructor to one of friendship. Mr James' fiancée, a lady referred to in the letter as Pam, appears to have been one of the operatives who received and decoded radio transmissions purportedly sent by Lauwers from behind enemy lines in the Netherlands. An interesting point the letter discloses is that at the time all radio transmissions from SOE agents in the field were initially handled and decoded by SIS (MI6), before then being passed on to the SOE. This was a period of time when radio training, communications and decoding of incoming messages from agents in the field, came under the control of the SIS.

Pam noticed that Lauwers' security check was missing from his radio transmissions, as was 'the usual JIMPAM' from the 'jumbled letters used to make code-breaking more difficult'. Although Mr James also noted on the 'station log' that 'the operator was not normal', the only action taken by their superiors was to reprimand them both. Afterwards Pam saw no more radio transmissions from Lauwers, the assumption being that future messages were sent direct from the radio station (in the Netherlands) to London and not through the decoding department where Mr James and Pam worked.

This letter certainly clears up one point which has been a bone of contention in relation to Operation North Pole for many years; if there was any wrongdoing or cover up over whether or not British authorities knew that their agents had been compromised, then this was carried out by SIS and not the SOE.

Contained within the file held by the SOE on Lauwers are a number of letters and reports which cover the topic of whether or not the British intelligence services believed he had actively and willingly co-operated with the Germans, or whether his actions were simply down to nothing more sinister than being hoodwinked by his interrogators. These letters and reports are very detailed and make for an interesting read, and the file also includes a statement made by Lauwers when he was held at Special Training School 28 at Tyting House, Guildford, after his return to England at the end of the war. It is dated 30 May 1945 and covers the time from when he was dropped into the Netherlands on the evening of 7 November 1941, until his eventual return to England on 21 May 1945. Lauwers began the statement by explaining that he and his fellow SOE agent, Thijs Taconis, had been tasked to start the organisation of the Dutch underground movement and to try to make contact with two other SOE agents, code named 'AB' and 'COR', who had been dropped into Holland in September 1941 and whose return to England was overdue. Lauwers and Taconis eventually located 'AB', who it turned out had been arrested by the

Gestapo, but managed to escape from Scheveningen prison where he was been held.

Lauwers' statement also makes reference to a commanding officer, Major Giesekens, this is clearly a reference to the chief of German military intelligence Section IIIF, Hermann Giskes. He was treated reasonably well whilst a prisoner of the Germans, during which time he made every attempt to notify London of his plight, even though his messages were, sadly, misunderstood.

The statement finishes with Lauwers explaining that he was liberated by the Russians from Rathenow concentration camp on 26 April 1945. He died in Utrecht on 13 June 2004.

Lauwers was recommended for the Military Medal on 5 November 1942, some eight months after his capture and arrest by the Germans. Most, if not all, of the examples of good work carried out by Lauwers to prove his worthiness of the award of the Military Medal were whilst he was a captive of the Germans.

Lauwers' fellow agent, Thijs Taconis, was born in Rotterdam on 28 March 1914. As a young man his education culminated in him studying mathematics and physics at Leiden University. Taconis also had a flair for languages, being able to speak English, German and French, in addition to his mother tongue.

Wanting to do his bit to help free his nation from the grip of Nazi control, Taconis made his way to England where he became an official in the Dutch Ministry of Defence, working out of Stratton House in London, between 1 June 1940 and 1 January 1941. He then made his way to Canada, where he enlisted in the Royal Dutch Army on 15 January and became a private soldier. Two months later, on 27 March, he returned to Britain to begin his training as an agent with the SOE on 28 May.

A report written about him by a Colonel Johnston, dated 17 June 1941, included the following remarks.

Fieldcraft: Slow but works well.
Weapons: He is a fair shot with all weapons. Slow and very deliberate. He understands all weapons he has been taught to use.
Explosives: Very deliberate and capable.

Communications: Has done well and can read and send 8 words a minute.
Map Reading: Has shown great interest and understands map reading. Field sketching very good.
Driving, etc: Bicycle, motor car.
Remarks: Place in Category A. Physically fit, but not strong. Well educated. A good type. Has character, is quiet, sensible and appears entirely trustworthy and reliable. His knowledge of, and his activities in the Dutch Youth Movement for the past 5 years, could make him a useful organiser amongst this movement, in which he could contact staunch supporters. Has done well here.

It would appear from Colonel Johnston's report that not only was Taconis a very capable individual, and more than suited for life as an SOE agent, he was also very well thought of.

A further report on Taconis, dated 1 July 1941, was written by Corporal Mendes, a member of the training staff at STS 21:

After Rolfs, one of the most reliable men we've got. There is nothing problematic about him. He will speak up frankly when something is on his mind. Knows how to keep things simple and well-ordered. Is very competent at all subjects, especially when chosen as leader for a military scheme. He's ideal moreover to become a professional soldier after the war. Knows quite a lot about chemistry.

Having been parachuted into the Netherlands on 7 November 1941, along with fellow SOE operative Huub Lauwers, Taconis was captured by the Germans on 9 March 1942 after being betrayed by fellow dutchman, Johannes Mattheus de Droog. He was sent to Mauthausen, where he was executed on 6 September 1944.

In Taconis' SOE file are a number of letters, dated between April and June 1943, in relation to him having been awarded the Military Medal. One of the letters is dated 30 June and was sent from the Foreign Office in London to Brigadier F.C. Curtis at the War Office. The letter is signed by a T.N. Dicker and marked 'SECRET'.

Dear Brigadier Curtis,

Many thanks for your letter DDMO/BM/272 of 24th June, about the presentation of the Military Medal to Private Thijs Taconis, of the Netherlands Army.

We quite appreciate the reasons for secrecy in this matter, and in our despatch to our Ambassador to the Netherlands, a copy of which I enclose for your information, you will see that we have merely notified The King's approval of the award and have refrained from any allusion to the question of arrangements for presentation of the Medal to Taconis.

Yours sincerely

T.N. Dicker.

The number of letters exchanged, and in particular their dates, is very interesting. What is not made clear throughout the exchange, though, is why Taconis was recommended for the award and not other SOE personnel who had undertaken similar dangerous work in the field.

The third paragraph of the official recommendation for the award of the Military Medal for Taconis read as follows:

At our request TACONIS planned and organised, in June 1942, an attack on the German radio station at KOOTWIJK. There is every reason to suppose that this attack would have been successful had the assault party not come upon land-mines, the presence of which was not expected, and roused the guard, with resultant failure. TACONIS' organisation has neither been shaken nor endangered in any way by this incident, thus affording proof of the efficient way in which his work has been done.

The major problem with this paragraph is that Taconis had been arrested by the German authorities on 9 March 1942, three months before this raid is supposed to have taken place. It can only be assumed that after having been captured, and whilst been held in captivity, Taconis sent radio messages back to London informing them of raids and other similar incidents he had been involved in and/ or carried out, under instruction of German intelligence officers.

The recommendation for the Military Medal to Taconis was made by Brigadier Colin Gubbins, chief of the SOE, based on information which it appears was received from Taconis in the guise of supposedly freely sent radio transmissions, but which it now transpires were after he had already been arrested and detained by the Germans.

It is unclear as to what Taconis did and did not actually do whilst operating as an SOE agent behind enemy lines, because it appears that what he is credited with was derived from information taken from messages he sent back to Britain. The question is, had he been captured before or after the messages had been sent?

Here are some of the claims made in relation to Taconis' achievements. He carried out valuable work in helping to set up local resistance movements. In total he set up and helped train ten saboteur groups each consisting of eight men. Each of the groups was located in a different area of the Netherlands and did their best to be as troublesome as they could, whilst at the same time trying not to draw too much attention to their activities. It was a fine line to tread; a balancing act between carrying out acts of sabotage that would be of a nuisance to the Germans, but relatively minor in scale so as not to evoke acts of retaliation against the civilian population.

Taconis also organised reception committees to await the arrival of weapons and munitions dropped in metal containers by aircraft of the RAF at designated drop sites throughout the Netherlands. These were shared out amongst the different resistance groups and then hidden away until they were required at a later date. This was in the period of time before Operation North Pole began, when it was possible for such deliveries to be made before the Germans were in place waiting to gather up agents and supplies that had been dropped by parachute.

Before his capture by the Germans, Taconis proved to be an extremely effective agent and an excellent example of the work which could have been carried out by the captured agents who came after him if the Germans had not known of their impending arrival.

The work carried out by Taconis and the members of the resistance groups he had put in place also included gathering relevant information about the German occupying forces, including their units, numbers, location, equipment, and even down to any atrocities they had carried out. Knowledge of documents such as identity cards, both Dutch and German military ones, or ration books, what colour they were and the specific wording printed in them was important, not only so that this information could be sent back to Britain, but so that forgeries could be made as well. Such forgeries had to be of an excellent quality to fool the Germans, because being found in possession of such an item could result in dire consequences for the individual concerned.

On one occasion, Taconis and a number of men from one of his groups were awaiting the arrival of an SOE agent. Unfortunately, the man badly injured himself when landing in the dark and despite receiving medical attention, died just a few days later. Taconis arranged for the man to be buried at night and in such a way that left no obvious sign of a grave, thus ensuring that the Germans never discovered the remains. This also prevented them knowing there was an active resistance cell operating in the area.

Taconis' Military Medal was presented to his father on 11 November 1947. The citation for the award read as follows:

> Sergeant Thijs Taconis was landed in Holland by parachute, with a wireless operator, early in November 1941 after which he did valuable and notable work both in performing the tasks he was originally despatched and in many other ways.
>
> Taconis organised and trained 10 groups of saboteurs, each group consisting of an average of 8 men. These groups were situated in various parts of Holland and were active, but unobtrusive in the sabotage of enemy transport, acts of arson were also undertaken.
>
> In June 1942, at our request, Taconis planned and organised an attack on the German radio station at Kootwijk. There is every reason to suppose that this attack would have been successful had the assault party not come upon land mines, the presence of which was unknown, and roused the

guards when a few of them were detonated. This resulted in the failure of the operation. Taconis' organisation were neither shaken nor endangered in any way by this incident, thus affording proof of the efficient way in which his work had been done.

With the aid of reception committees organised locally by Taconis, 10 deliveries of stores compromising in all 52 containers were made. The total net weight of these stores exceeded 5 tons and they were distributed amongst the various sabotage reception committees, under the guidance of Taconis. At different times he provided safe accommodation to 8 officers and other ranks proceeding to the field, whose chances of safety and the ultimate success of whose work depended to an important extent on the services this rendered. In fact, it was due to the assistance in the initial stages of Taconis and his men, that plans for the organisation of resistance groups in Holland were completed so rapidly.

One of the officers whom Taconis received was unfortunate enough to suffer severe concussion on landing. He was none the less safely housed, given medical attention and finally, when after a few days he died, buried clandestinely and therefore without danger to the organisation.

Many other services were rendered by Taconis and his helpers in the way of receiving special equipment and messages and passing them through to other agents in the field, and even latterly in obtaining valuable information in regard to the issue of identity and ration cards in Holland.

Throughout all these months of active and intelligent planning and organisation, Taconis was in constant danger, the nature and extent of which can only be surmised, but which by his high degree of courage, resourcefulness and devotion to duty, he successfully combatted.

His work commanded the unreserved respect of all who had experience of such activities.

On 2 May 1953, Taconis was posthumously awarded the Bronze Cross by the Dutch authorities. The citation for that read as follows:

Sergeant Thijs Taconis distinguished himself by courageous action against the enemy as an agent of a secret intelligence service, which during the years 1940-1945 sent him into enemy occupied territory, where he had a life-threatening task to perform under extremely difficult circumstances, which eventually led to his death through enemy counter action.

Taconis was undoubtedly an extremely brave young man who took a number of calculated risks, despite knowing that his actions could lead to him being arrested, interrogated, tortured and even killed by the Germans.

9 December 1941

Willem Jacobus van der Reyden was born on 16 February 1915 in Rotterdam. During his training, he also used the alias surname of Reijden and the code name of 'Rover'. He landed at the coastal town of Scheveningen, a district of The Hague, via a Royal Navy motor torpedo boat on the evening of 9 December 1941. Although his arrival was during the time of Operation North Pole, he was an agent of MI6 and not the SOE, which is possibly the reason why the Gestapo were not waiting for him on his arrival. He remained at large for more than two months before he was arrested on 13 February 1942.

During the rest of the war, van der Reyden was held at a number of different camps, eventually ending up at Sachsenhausen. He was one of the 3,400 inmates still being held at the camp when they were liberated on 22 April 1945 by elements of the Soviet Union's 1st Belorussian Front, and the 2nd Polish Infantry Division.

On his return to Britain, and just seven months after having been liberated, he married Gwendoline Margaret Brewis on 8 November 1945, with the couple's wedding certificate showing Willem's profession as wireless operator. In 1954, van der Reyden, who at the time was living in Norwich, was issued with his certificate of naturalisation, officially making him a British citizen.

Agents Captured During
Operation North Pole - 1942

The dropping of SOE agents into the Netherlands continued into 1942. Not only was there a massive increase in the number of drops from the previous year, being eighteen in total, the number of agents involved also increased, numbering thirty-six. Operation North Pole was well and truly underway.

23 February 1942

Evert Radema and Ernst Willem de Jonge were both MI6 agents and are good examples of the very confusion highlighted earlier surrounding exactly who was part of Operation North Pole and who was not. Despite both men being operatives of MI6, Radema's name is one of those recorded on a memorial erected at Mauthausen by the Dutch War Grave Foundation to commemorate the names of forty-seven Dutch and British special agents who were murdered at the camp between 6 and 7 September 1944.

Radema was born on 7 August 1903 in Foxhol, Hoogezand. After completing his secondary education, he attended the nautical school in Amsterdam with the intention of joining the Merchant Navy. After having successfully completed his course, in 1933 he went to work for the Dutch shipping company Maatschappij Netherland as a radio operator.

At the outbreak of the Second World War, Radema's ship just happened to be in a British port and was unable to return to the Netherlands. With his wife and children waiting for him back home, he was approached by the Dutch Central Intelligence and asked if he would consider working for them, which he agreed to do, and was then trained by MI6 to become a spy. During his training he used the alias surname of Brewers.

Radema was arrested on 29 May 1942 in Amsterdam, where he had been since at least April, and at the time of his arrest was in possession of his radio transmitter. German military intelligence attempted to force him to make contact with London, but when he failed to enter the required security check into his message, MI6 did not reply. This adds confusion into the equation of the SOE not apparently recognising similar omissions in messages sent by their agents during the same time frame.

Radema was initially held and interrogated at the local police station before being moved to the prison camp used by the SD at the old seminary building at Haaren, where he remained until being moved to another camp at Assen, along with several other prisoners, in November 1943. Five months later, on 30 April 1944, Radema was moved again, this time to a camp at Rawicz, before ending up at Mauthausen, where he arrived on 6 September, and was killed later the same day.

The death record book for Mauthausen records that the reason for Radema's arrest had been '*Schutz*' (protective custody). His profession was shown as a '*Funker*' (radio operator), and that his cause of death was '*auf der flucht erschossen*' (shot while escaping). He was posthumously awarded the (Dutch) Queen's Commendation for Bravery in 1947, and the Bronze Cross the following year.

Ernst Willem de Jonge, meanwhile, was born on 22 May 1914 in Sinabang, Indonesia. Before the war he had worked as a lawyer but was also an Olympian, having taken part as a rower at the 1936 summer Olympics in Berlin. At the outbreak of the Second World War, he had volunteered for the Dutch resistance, before making his way to England, where he arrived in London on 31 August 1941. Initially interrogated by the British Secret Service, he was asked if he would work as agent in German-occupied Holland. He was trained by MI6 in Morse code and decoding in London.

Although the initial plan had been to parachute Radema and de Jonge into Holland, in the end they were taken across the English Channel by a motor torpedo boat, before canoeing the last half mile or so onto the beach at Katwijk aan Zee. Later that morning, the pair caught a tram to Leiden and went their separate ways: Radema to Amsterdam and de Jonge to Wassenaar, a coastal town in South Holland, where he made contact with the Dutch resistance. He then moved on to Rotterdam, where he set up a spy ring which focused on gathering information useful to the Allies.

A member of de Jonge's group was captured by the Gestapo on 22 May 1942 on his way to England. In his possession he had three rolls of microfilm, one of which included a detailed report written by de Jonge, who was then arrested three days later in an apartment in Rotterdam, alongside two of his colleagues. After he was interrogated, he spent time in a number of concentration camps before eventually ending up at Rawicz. The prison did not have a particularly good reputation; 886 people died there during the war simply because of its harsh conditions. He was murdered there on 3 September 1944, and his remains were never recovered.

28 February 1942

Georgius Petrus Wilhelmus 'Gerrit' Dessing was born in Naaldwijk, on 26 January 1910, and as a young man had worked as an accountant for Curry, Caruthers & Thompson, an accountancy firm in Johannesburg, South Africa.

Having made his way to England after the fall of the Netherlands in May 1940, he joined the Dutch Army in London on 20 August and worked at their headquarters at Stratton House. He later agreed to work for the SOE by returning to his homeland. As an SOE agent he went by the names of George Peter William Dirksen (the name used during his weeks of training), George Dircksen, Gerrit Dekkers, and Gerrit van den Broek. His official code name, however, was 'Carrot'.

Initial observations about Dessing by training staff at STS 4, the preliminary school for the SOE's Dutch and Belgian sections, on 19 May 1941 included comments that he was physically strong, well-educated and well-travelled, keen, shrewd, humorous, popular and doing well.

Just two days later, the station's commanding officer in charge of the training, Lieutenant Colonel Johnston, further noted that Dessing was 'a good type, had character, was quiet, sensible and able to look after himself and appears to be entirely trustworthy and reliable. Is anxious to do a job and would not mind what he is asked to do. Would make a good leader or organiser.'

Dessing's SOE file stretches to nearly 100 pages, not all of which are positive and/or complimentary, suggesting that initial observations made about him were not a good judgement of his true character. It is actually quite remarkable that he was ever deployed as an agent behind enemy lines as it appears that in July 1941, he found himself in trouble for drink-related matters and ended up in the 'Cooler' (military gaol) for his behaviour, which in civilian life would have been the equivalent of being sent to prison.

The detention centre in question is not actually named, but it would not have been an established military one due to concerns that he might talk about his personal circumstances, and that he was undergoing training as an agent; not something the SOE, military authorities, or Winston Churchill, for that matter, would be happy to become common knowledge.

According to Dessing's official SOE file, he arrived at the detention centre on 24 July 1941, just two months after he had begun his initial training with the Special Operations Executive.

Report on reasons for going to the Cooler
Arrived: 24 July 1941.
Reasons: (a). Lack of self-control; agent freely on drink; formed sentimental attachments with women when intoxicated.

(b). His lack of control considered by the Dutch section to endanger his colleagues.

(c). His fellow students profoundly distrust him.

These reasons were qualified by a statement to the affect that he might be useful as a guide for a raiding party.

Dirksen pulled himself together in the Cooler. His general behaviour was excellent.

Disposal: Returned to Country Section for employment.

He was very glad indeed to go into the world again, after having endured his stay here with great patience. He was released on 4 October 1941.

Despite being released to continue his training as an SOE agent, there was a discussion as to whether an application should be made to dispense with his services, but the decision was taken to let him continue his training.

The initial intention was for him to be dropped on the night of 28 February 1942 by parachute near the Belgian town of Houthalen, but whether by mistake or enemy ground fire, he ended up being dropped more than 100 miles away in Ermelo, in the Dutch province of Gelderland, an event which undoubtedly saved his life as there was no Gestapo reception committee waiting for him. As he was sent to carry out specific assignments in the Netherlands, it is unclear as to why the initial intention had been to drop him into Belgium, but his mission was to locate and assist the Dutch former Prime Minister Hendrikus Colijn and Minister of War Jannes Johannes Cornelis van Dijk to escape from the Netherlands. Unfortunately, Dessing was unable to help either man as both had already been arrested by the time of his arrival.

He had also been tasked with setting up a team of saboteurs in the Dordecht and Rotterdam areas in relation to German shipping that used both ports extensively. Having completed his mission as best he could, Dessing decided that it was time to return to London. This makes him rather unique in so far as despite being dropped into the German-occupied Netherlands, he actually managed to escape capture and make his way back to England, arriving in London on 2 September 1943 using a route which took him via Brussels and Gibraltar.

Dessing's SOE file included the following note that was dated 2 December 1943, three months after his return:

Alias G. Dirkson, arrived in UK from Gibraltar on 2.9.43. Regarding the matter of disposal of this student was in the field from February 42 to September 43, and that since his return he has not re-entered training. It has been agreed that there is no need for him to be further interviewed and a disposal form can be put through immediately for the consideration of recommending his transfer to employment with the Dutch government.

It is considered definitely impossible to use this man again as an agent in the field as he is most probably 'blown' there. Work has been offered him in the Dutch government which it is considered to be the best solution. It has been arranged that he will start work on 6 December 1943 in a civilian capacity.

He is a stupid type of man. I cannot think that he will be secure. He is too unintelligent.

There is an even more interesting and potentially explosive note contained within Dessing's SOE file, dated 7 June 1945, which again relates to Dessing's actions and behaviour as an agent. It was sent to somebody with the initials LC, and was from somebody with the initials D/LA:

Early in 1942 we sent an agent into Holland on the carrot operation (the agent was known as George Dircksen). He was sent on the suggestion of Max Sluyser (a Dutch press official) to contact a prominent Social Democrat and Trade Unionist named LJ van Looij. The agent stayed with van Looij for some time and then returned to this country through France and Portugal.

Max Sluyser phoned me at my private address on Tuesday to say he had been in Holland and met van Looij, who had spent several months in a German concentration camp. He said that van Looij attributed his troubles with the Gestapo to the afore mentioned agent, and Sluyser suggested meeting me to give me the details.

I told Sluyser that it was some years since I had anything to do with the matter and that I was not prepared to act as intermediary, having practically left the organisation, and that he must find another channel if he wished the matter to be taken up.

I am letting you know this in case the matter should be raised with you through another channel.

There were a few notes which had been handwritten on the bottom of the page, not all of which were legible, but one of them said the following: 'N [Dutch section] concerned that story told on return not complete and possible not all correct. Impossible to prove either way.' Neither the typed content of the note, nor the handwritten additions at the bottom of the page, reflected particularly well on Dessing and his reputation, leaving uncertainty and doubt as to why he might not have been completely honest about his actions.

The information contained within the file includes Dessing's interrogation on his return to Britain, and a number of cipher telegrams between London and Bern, Switzerland, mainly from 1943. It also includes the fact that Dessing was arrested and imprisoned for eight days whilst he was in France, having been stopped by French police in St. Julien and found to be in possession of false documentation.

After the war, Dessing settled in Johannesburg and began working as an accountant. He lived to the age of 75, passing away on 28 September 1985.

On 2 May 1953, he was awarded both the Dutch Bronze Cross and the Airman's Cross for his wartime efforts. The citations for the two awards were as follows:

Bronze Cross
He has distinguished himself in the face of the enemy as an agent of a secret intelligence group that had dispatched him in February 1942 to enemy held territory where he had to perform a death defying task under extremely trying circumstances. Subsequently he managed to evade capture

by diverting to Switzerland, taking incriminating material with him.

Airman's Cross

He has distinguished himself in connection with hostile action by courageous and tactful conduct and so serving the interests of the Kingdom, after he had been dropped by parachute as an agent of a secret intelligence service in the Netherlands, having performed a death defying task under extremely trying circumstances, he has escaped to Switzerland and without hesitation tried to reach England, on his way through France he was arrested but managed to escape after two weeks and subsequently arrived safely in London after six months via the Pyrenees and Spanish prisons.

It is interesting to note that when Dessing returned to Britain, he was not arrested, nor did he spend time in prison whilst the British authorities determined whether they believed he was a double agent, which was the complete opposite of how Pieter Dourlein, who had discovered the operation had been compromised, was treated when he returned. Dourlein, a Dutchman, had escaped from the Netherlands in 1941, making his way across the North Sea to England in a motorboat. The following year he joined the SOE and in March 1943 was dropped back into the Netherlands, where he was immediately captured by the Germans. Along with another captured SOE agent, Johan Ubbink, he managed to escape on the evening of 29 August 1943, with both men eventually arriving back in England on 1 February 1944. Suspected of being German spies, they were arrested and imprisoned for four months before being released.

12 March 1942

On 12 March 1942, three agents from MI6/Dutch Intelligence were dropped by a motor patrol boat off the Dutch coast at Katwijk. The three men were Felix Dono Ortt, Jan Emmer and Armand Guillaume Henri Maassen.

Felix Dono Ortt was born on 21 January 1907 in Nijmegen. Before the outbreak of war, he was a Lieutenant 3rd Class in the Koninklijke Marine and had been part of an Allied transatlantic convoy that was attacked by the German submarine *U-101* on 19 October 1940, some 100 miles north-west of Barra Head in the Outer Hebrides.

After Germany's occupation of his country, he made his way to England in the latter part of 1940 and was recruited by MI6. After completing his training, he was dropped into the Netherlands on the evening of 12 March 1942, but did not remain at large for long, being arrested on 23 May. As Ortt was not arrested immediately after his arrival, it is questionable as to whether or not he was actually part of Operation North Pole, but his position as an agent of British military intelligence who was dropped into the Netherlands between 1942 and 1944, and who was subsequently murdered by the Germans whilst being held in captivity, means his inclusion here adds value to the overall story. The other consideration to take into account is that the different sides more than likely classed agents sent and captured differently from one another. Having said that, it is noticeable that although tasked to undertake similar roles, the Germans often were only in place to capture SOE agents rather than those sent by MI6, which in turn could also suggest that the Germans had a spy working with the SOE but not in MI6.

On 30 June 1942, Ortt was moved to the SD prison in Haaren, under the name of Albert Overbeek. Where that name came from is unclear, but more than likely it was of German design so as to hide the fact that Ortt had been captured and taken prisoner. There was great value to be gained by a combatant nation if they did not acknowledge they had captured or killed an enemy agent. That way they could take their time to decide the best way to use the individual concerned. If nothing else, such a tactic caused confusion and uncertainty, especially if the agent had been tasked with carrying out specific actions once behind enemy lines.

On 27 November 1943, Ortt was transferred to the Huis van Bewaring prison in Assen. How long he was actually incarcerated there is unclear, but it is known that by 30 April 1944 he was being held at Rawicz under his own name, along with fifty other Allied agents.

Despite the fact that Ortt's name was still shown on the prison's records as late as 3 September 1944, it is interesting that the Dutch War Grave Foundation have officially recorded his date of death as being 30 April 1944, even though it is not actually known when or where he died, or whether he has any known grave. On 6 June 1953 he was posthumously awarded the Dutch Bronze Cross for his 'services as a secret agent in occupied territory during the years 1943 and 1944.'

Jan Emmer was born on 6 April 1917 in Wormer. He left the Netherlands around midnight on 17 September 1941 with four other Dutchmen, H.J. Schilp, J.R. Morré, R.E. Sanders and Armand de Jong, setting sail for England from the Dutch coast at Callantsoog in a boat powered by an outboard engine. On 19 September they ran out of petrol so with no more use for the engine, they simply threw it overboard. This left them completely vulnerable as now their only option was to row, making their time at sea much longer than they had anticipated, and more vulnerable to enemy aircraft. Fortunately, just a few hours after having jettisoned their engine, they came across HMT *Solon*, a British minesweeping trawler, and were taken on board and carried to Great Yarmouth.

After arriving in England, Emmer was approached by Dutch intelligence and MI6 and asked if he would be prepared to return to the Netherlands to take part in clandestine operations against German forces. He readily agreed.

Emmer's first job was to locate the Dutch politician, Johannes (Hans) Linthorst Homan, along with some senior Dutch naval officers, and return with them to England. Unfortunately for Emmer, on the day of his return to the Netherlands, the Abwehr began Operation North Pole, which meant that German forces in occupied Holland were on heightened alert for enemy spies. However, it was more a case of British incompetence, rather than due diligence on the German's part that led to Emmer's eventual arrest. The money he had been given to cover his expenses and living costs whilst in the Netherlands was out of date and no longer legal tender. Worse than that, the Dutch identity card he had been given was of extremely poor quality and clearly stood out when looked at next to the real thing.

Once landed at Katwijk, he managed to stay at large for some ten weeks before being captured on 30 May 1942 in Rotterdam after having been betrayed by a Dutch traitor posing as agent of MI6. He was conveyed to the prison camp at the old seminary at Haaren, where he arrived the following day. He was later moved on to the prison camp at Rawicz before ending up at Mauthausen, where he was murdered between 6 and 7 September 1944.

Finally, Armand Guillaume Henri Maassen was born on 3 January 1920 at Maastricht. After escaping from the Netherlands following the occupation, he escaped and made his way to England, where he arrived on 27 September 1941.

Sometime after his arrival, he enlisted in the British Royal Navy and became a seaman 1st Class. He became involved in dropping off secret agents along the Dutch coastline; the very work he was involved in on 12 March 1942. Unfortunately for him, after dropping off Emmer and Ortt, the surf was too strong and he was unable to row back to the waiting MTB. Stranded on the beach, he made his way into Katwijk seeking help from some friendly locals, but the next morning he was betrayed (although by then the rubber dingy he had left on the beach had also been discovered), and he was arrested by the Germans. He was initially held at the prisoner of war camp at Wilhelmshaven, before being moved to another camp at Amersfoort, where he died from pneumonia on 10 February 1943. It had initially been believed that Maassen was a secret agent who had been dropped off along with other agents. The truth eventually came to light when a fellow prisoner at Amersfoort, P.J. de Lint, recanted the true story of how Maassen came to be on the beach at Katwijk, which had been told to him by Maassen himself.

27 March 1942

Arnoldus Albert 'Nol' Baatsen was born in Amsterdam on 11 April 1918. Prior to the war he had been a photographer in civilian life, which was far removed from what he did for his country during his involvement in the Second World War.

Having enlisted in the Dutch Army, he was part of the Coastal Artillery as a range finder between 2 November 1937 and 7 October 1938. He was fully mobilised on 11 April 1939, and after having escaped to England, he served with the Dutch Royal Army in London from 15 April 1940. In May 1941 he became a member of the SOE and was given the code name of 'Watercress'. Whilst undergoing his training to become an agent, he used the surname of Bouwman, and his area of expertise became that of sabotage. It was common practice for perspective agents to use a different surname during their training, quite possibly because not all those who took part in this stage of training were deemed suitable and subsequently did not complete the course. Not knowing a fellow student's name simply provided another layer of security for all concerned.

The following are examples of just a few of the reports made about Baatsen during his training with the SOE. These reports, however minimal they might appear, were extremely important as they would ultimately determine if an individual had the required skill set and was of a sufficient standard to be deployed as an agent behind enemy lines. It was not enough just to be patriotic and 'OK' at one particular aspect of the work. If an agent did not have the all-round capabilities to be able to operate effectively and survive in the field, they could be a danger not only to themselves, but those they were working alongside as well.

17 June 1941 – Colonel Johnston

Physically fit and strong. Well educated and intelligent. Appears reliable and trustworthy. Good spirit and patriotic. Somewhat lacking in character. Has done well at the school. Has intimate knowledge of the City Electric Works in Amsterdam, which supplies power for Fokker Aeroplane Factories. He could be usefully employed amongst the 2,000 workmen there, many of whom he knows, for propaganda and sabotage work and I think would do well. Would make a good instructor.

7 July 1941 – Corporal Mendes

He and Winsdaal are the type, that although inspired by the best patriotic motives, require immediate action and anything which does not conform with his conception of constant move, and its interpretation in terms of action, as mere stagnation. Therefore, not the best type for underground work.

21 July 1941 – Corporal Mendes

The 'he-man' type; well-built, physically well developed, with a flair for subjects involving alertness or sensation; unarmed combat, demolitions and para-military stuff in general. Not so good when purely mental qualities must be exerted.

The following report was sent by an unnamed instructor or officer and was sent for the information of the officer in charge of STS 6:

4 November 1941 – To officer commanding STS 6

The following report about Bouwman has been received from the Administration Officer at Station XVII and is for your information. He was given weekend leave to proceed to Cambridge, 1 November 1941. He was seen 2 November 1941 in the Salisbury Hotel, Hertford with a female companion who he introduced as a friend from London. I have seen Bouwman indicated the seriousness of this action from the security point of view. He insisted he had been to Cambridge, although I inferred he had not. He is leaving for Station VI today and I have given him instructions that he is not to repeat the offence.

This final report is an example of an agent's inability to fully grasp the enormity of what exactly it was they were being trained to do, and of the impending situation they would shortly find themselves in, where such mistakes could literally cost them their lives.

From the reports written about Baatsen by those who were involved in his training, it would be fair to describe him as a 'mistake waiting to happen'. By Christmas of 1941, because of an undisclosed incident, serious consideration was given to sending him to the Cooler. He was in further trouble for giving out his name, as well as the address of the SOE training establishment he was attending, to a woman he had meant whilst on a night out.

A typed, but unsigned, report about Baatsen dated 21 January 1942 brought into question his suitability to become an agent with the SOE:

This man's life history will be as his own up to the moment the Dutch Army capitulated.

At that time Baatsen was in London. In the confusion of the moment, he decided that now he had a chance to disappear, as if he was missed, everybody in Holland would think that he had either been killed, or gone to England, and the troops in England would think he had stayed behind in Holland.

His reason for wanting to disappear was that his wife was trying to divorce him and that during the process he had to pay her £1.12 a week. This, of course, cramped his style considerably, and he therefore intended to make himself scarce.

While serving in the Army in Ymuiden, he kept some civilian clothes in a pub, where he was in the habit of changing when he wanted to travel to Amsterdam for the purpose of seeing one of his many girlfriends without the formality of a leave pass or other authorisation.

That day, 15th May, there were dozens of abandoned motor cars standing around in Ymuiden where owners had escaped to England. He took one of these and drove to Amsterdam, where he went underground in a very cheap labourer's hotel, moving in with a policeman's family as an unofficial boarder shortly after. (Bouwman will have to supply name and address himself.)

Since that time, he lived by making money on the black market in Amsterdam, and by taking to odd jobs.

A short time ago he almost met his wife in the street, but managed to dodge through an alley in time. This near calamity made him decide to leave Amsterdam at once and he moved to The Hague, where he is now looking for work.

The following was part of a report that had been written about Baatsen on 24 January 1942, along with what looks to be a reply that is dated 26 January 1942:

It would appear that it is the intention of N section to use this man on a project in the near future. I feel that I must bring to your notice the fact that Bouwman has been reported to us on many occasions for extreme lack of discretion. I suggest that you should be satisfied that the importance of the project entrusted to Bouwman, justifies this risk.

I am very doubtful if it is wise to use a man who has such a poor security record and seems to be a foolish, theatrical and boastful type.

The concerns surrounding Baatsen's suitability to be an effective agent were so strong that even after the decision was taken for him to be dropped into the Netherlands, it was decided that he would work alone, without a wireless operator. This was mainly because students who had completed the same course as him had absolutely no confidence in him at all, and it was felt that none of them would have any desire to work with him.

He was finally dropped into the Netherlands on the evening of 27 March 1942, near Kallenkote, and was immediately arrested by the Gestapo who were waiting for him on the ground. He had been tasked with carrying out a number of assignments on his arrival, including destroying the headquarters of the German liaison service at the Hotel Aurora. Another target was a large fuel dump at Ypenburg airport, located in Rijswijk, which had only been completed in 1936. After the Dutch surrender to German forces, the airport was used by the Luftwaffe and subsequently attacked so frequently by the RAF that it was eventually put out of action, which raises the question of why Baatsen was tasked with destroying the airfield's fuel dumps.

Another of Baatsen's targets was a clothing and storage facility located in the Dutch village of Rijnsburg. The only possible relevance of this is that it must have been involved in the manufacturing of German uniforms and other military related items.

The time between Baatsen joining the SOE and being dropped into the Netherlands was just 127 days. He was initially interrogated by Giskes' assistant, Joseph Schreider, and held at different locations in the Netherlands before arriving at the seminary at Haaren on 1 May 1942, thirty-four days after he was arrested. He remained there until 27 November 1943, before being moved to Mauthausen, where he was murdered on 7 September 1944.

29 March 1942

This date is interesting as it saw four SOE agents dropped near the village of Holten in the Dutch province of Overijssel. Jan Molenaar, Leonard Theodoris Cornelis Andringa, Gozewijn Hendrik Gerard 'Gosse' Ras and Hendrik Johan Jordaan were not captured on the same day they landed, indicating that the Germans had maybe not been aware of their arrival.

Jan Molenaar was born on 12 March 1918 at Waddinxveen, near Gouda. He was one of nine children, having four brothers and three sisters. Prior to making his way to England after the Netherlands had fallen to German forces, he had served in the Dutch Army as a Corporal in the 2nd Hussar Regiment, which had seen him stationed at both The Hague and Amersfoort between February 1938 and August 1939. He then spent a further nine months serving in the Dutch mounted police.

He began his service with the SOE to become a wireless operator on 9 June 1941, and was granted a special commission at the rank of 2nd Lieutenant, using the alias surname of Maartens. On 5 June the SOE had been informed by Captain Kruls of the Dutch Army that he would not, in fact, be joining them, although there was no reason given as to why this was. Despite this, Molenaar arrived to start his course on 9 June as had originally been arranged.

The file held on Molenaar by the SOE was a substantial one; some seventy-seven pages in total. The first comments about how he was doing on his course were dated 28 June 1941, about three weeks into his course, and were made by a Colonel Thornton:

> He is well disciplined and keen. He has shown himself a good and capable man in all subjects. He is a quiet and self-possessed type but has plenty of initiative and drive. He is also interested in world affairs in general. It was typical of him that he was the only one not to take the chance of a visit to Northampton when it was offered. He has been the most consistent student on the course.

Further comments were added to his file on 19 July by Sergeant Webb of STS 1's training team: 'Corporal Maartens is a regular soldier. Very good type of man indeed. He is intelligent, resourceful and interested in all of the subjects. Very promising pupil. Has a hatred of the Germans.'

Molenaar was seriously injured on landing after hitting a brick wall, breaking both his legs and back. His injuries were sufficiently bad enough for him to take the extremely brave and selfless decision to commit suicide by means of taking a cyanide pill he had on his person, rather than be captured alive by the Germans and risk revealing information about his operation under interrogation. The injuries he sustained were confirmed in a note on his SOE file, dated 1 September 1942, which is marked Most Secret. The only identification on the note is that it is from 'L/WAD' and appears to be signed with the initials SN, which are in red ink.

> GILGAL
> I have the following information on this subject. On March 28th the TURNIP and LETTUCE operations (Netherlands Section) were carried out but the W/T operator GILGAL, broke his legs and his back by hitting a stone wall on landing. In telegrams from the field, he was called JOHN.
>
> A note from Dansey of February 22nd stated that arrangements had been made for DAVID to send a small number of messages to London via GILGAL. I rather think DAVID is not our man, but the Netherlands Section will obviously know more about this.

This clearly indicates concerns as to the validity of the messages being sent by the individual referred to as 'DAVID'. This note is followed by a Minute Sheet dated 4 September 1942:

> GILGAL
> (1). GILGAL is the wireless operator for a group of SOE men in the provinces of Limburge and Brabant in Holland. The group consists of one head organiser, two sub-organisers and the wireless man.

(2). The original wireless operator, by name of Jan Maartens, who was sent out with the organiser, was accidently killed on landing. The organiser informed us at the time that all papers and incriminating evidence was burnt. He subsequently found a local operator who was tested by our wireless station and found satisfactory and was there upon employed to take Jan Maartens' place.

(3). I find it very difficult to believe that this service calls itself GILGAL. So far as I know, this name is only used by our wireless station and then only to refer to the particular operator.

(4). I would be very grateful if you could press the A.C.S.S. for more information as to the source and reliability of the information he has sent. As it stands it is extremely vague and it makes it very difficult for us to know what action should be taken.

(5). If it is genuine, it is obvious that a number of people must be warned. If it is merely hearsay, more harm is done by frightening the people in the field and making them suspicious of one another.

This is a very interesting document because not only is it the first time there has been any official concern put in writing over the transmissions being received from agents in the field behind enemy lines in the Netherlands, it shows that despite these concerns, the SOE continued to send more agents. Between the date of this document and the end of Operation North Pole in April 1944, twenty-seven more agents were dropped into the Netherlands, with every one of them being arrested as soon as they landed.

Leonard Theodoris Cornelis Andringa was born on 22 November 1913 in The Hague. Language-wise he had the potential to make a good agent as he could speak English and German, as well as his mother tongue. He finished his full-time education when he left Leiden University in July 1934, when he was 20 years of age. He remained at home for a further year before making his way to England towards the end of 1935. When war was declared on 3 September 1939, he decided to enlist in the Dutch Army at Porthcawl, Wales, at which time he had no previous military training.

He went on to become an agent with the SOE on 28 May 1941, and whilst undergoing his training in Scotland went by the name of Leo Akkerman. He was described as being keen and enthusiastic and was an average shot with all weapons, as well understanding the mechanisms of each one he used. He was an all-round, above average student. The SOE file on Andringa includes a number of reports written by some of his instructors and the course's commanding officers.

17 June 1941 – Lieutenant Colonel Johnston
Physically fit. Well educated, quite sensible and appears reliable and trustworthy. Very anxious to work for his country. Accustomed to handle and deal with men and able to look after himself. He seems confident that he can contact and organise reliable people around The Hague and Frisian Islands. He would probably be best working on his own and would prefer to do so.

1 July 1941 – Corporal Mendes
A calm rather close nature. Mixes very well with the others but I am convinced that he is very reserved towards strangers, especially noticeable in his former attitude towards one or two women acquaintances. Reserved, aloof, no wild and *'Apres moi le deluge'* ['after me, the flood': a nihilistic expression of indifference to whatever happens after one has died] to women chasing.

7 July 1941 – Corporal Mendes
Is extremely quiet, almost timid. He is the only one of the students that I still don't know anything about. It is just impossible to get behind him. He is extremely careful not to commit himself for a single moment. Should I have to make a judgment I prefer to assume that in the light of his future activities, this negative attitude is one of his best qualifications.

The last of these reports, written by Lieutenant Colonel Evans, and dated 11 July 1941, almost begs the question as to why Andringa was accepted as an SOE agent, and why he was deemed suitable to be sent out into the field: 'Rather disappointing as although he is fit and has average ability, he does not display any initiative or particular interest. Stolid, or else intensely reserved.'

Andringa remained at large for a month before he was captured in The Hague on 28 April 1942, after an unnamed woman provided information about him to the local German authorities. Although initially interrogated by Schreider at Haaren, it is also known that he was held at Rawicz before eventually arriving at Mauthausen on 27 November 1943, where was murdered on 6 September 1944. His name is included on the memorial to the Dutch and British special agents murdered there between 6 and 7 September 1944.

Gozewijn Hendrik Gerard Ras was born on 27 August 1914 in Amsterdam. He came from an affluent family which enabled him to attend the prestigious Cambridge University in England between 1936 and 1940, where he earned an MA in Economics. He also received a diploma in typewriting and bookkeeping.

Before the outbreak of the war, he had worked as a clerk at a well-known brewery company, and prior to that had worked in a Parisian bank, before moving on to a stockbrokers on Wall Street, where he was a bond clerk.

Having made his way to England on board a merchant cargo vessel after his country had been occupied by Germany, on 15 November 1940 Ras enlisted in the Royal Dutch Army in London, before transferring to the British Army in April 1941 and serving as a private in the 1st/5th Battalion, Sherwood Foresters. A month later, however, on 28 May, he enlisted in the SOE. During his training he used the name Gerard Rolfs, and as an active agent he chose the name Gerard Roelofs, with his code name being 'Rikky'.

The first report written about Ras was dated 17 June 1941 and was penned by Colonel Johnston:

Physically strong and fit. Highly educated and travelled. Has character, powers of leadership and is probably the best man here. Could move in good society. Keen and sensible and appears reliable and trustworthy and able to look after himself. Willing and anxious to do any work for the good of his country. A good organiser.

Ras was captured in Utrecht on 1 May 1942, meaning he had been at large for a total of thirty-three days following his arrival. After being interrogated by Abwehr officers, Ras spent time as a prisoner at Haaren, before arriving at Mauthausen on 27 November 1943, where he was executed by a bullet to the head on 7 September 1944.

Hendrik Johan Jordaan was born on 9 July 1918 in Haaksbergen, where his father worked as a textile manager. In his late teens he worked as an aeroplane mechanic and was an ardent hater of the Nazis. In 1937 he undertook seven months' military service with the Dutch Army, and then, like many of his compatriots following the Netherlands' capitulation to the Germans, made his way to England. He then joined the Royal Dutch Naval Air Service in August 1940, before going on to enlist in the SOE on 15 January 1942. Because of his height (6 feet 3 inches), he stood out from the crowd, which was not necessarily a good thing for somebody who wanted to become a secret agent.

Just five days into his training, however, he had already created a good impression amongst his instructors:

> Physically fit. A good type, quiet, serious and well educated. Has not much experience of life, appears thoroughly reliable. Has worked hard and done well and is very keen. Too young to be a leader. Is a good signaller. Can read and send 16 w.p.m and could easily be trained on wireless and be usefully employed as a communications agent. He is not as physically tough as the others on his course and is better theory wise than he is in a practical sense in most aspects of his training, although he is exceptionally good at Morse Code.

During his initial training with the SOE, he was given the courtesy rank of 2nd Lieutenant and went by the alias of Harry Jeffers. Having successfully passed his course and been posted to the SOE's Dutch Section N, he took on the name of Johan Roessingh, rather than reverting to his actual name, Jordaan. Having landed safely in the Netherlands, he managed to remain at large for a total of thirty-six days before being captured in Rotterdam on 3 May 1942. It would appear that the reason why he was not arrested immediately on landing was because he and his colleagues were accidentally dropped at the wrong location.

Jordaan spent time in Sachsenhausen concentration camp before eventually ending up in Mauthausen, where he died on 3 May 1945.

A fellow Dutchman by the name of C. Vrolijk was also a prisoner at Sachsenhausen and Mauthausen at the same time as Jordaan. Vrolijk survived the war and whilst being treated for pneumonia in Den Haag in October 1945, he gave an account of time they had spent together as prisoners. He explained how the two men were part of a group of 180 prisoners who were moved from Sachsenhausen to Mauthausen in what he described as 'railway wagons'. The journey took six days, during which time they neither ate or drank anything, and by the time they arrived, nine of their number were dead.

According to Vrolijk, on leaving Mauthausen, Jordaan was generally in good health, although he did have an open wound on one of his legs, which never seemed to improve; there was more chance of being fed than receiving medical treatment, but even that was a rarity. The camp was liberated on 5 May 1945, although that very morning 2,300 of the camp's inmates had been gassed. In the weeks leading up to the liberation, Jordaan's health had deteriorated dramatically, to such a degree that he was unable to stand up unless aided by others. He had very bad diarrhoea and even struggled to eat his meagre ration of bread.

On the evening of 2 May, Vrolijk, at great personal risk, made his way to the camp's kitchen and stole a couple briquettes of brown coal (effective at reducing the symptoms of diarrhoea), one of which he gave to Jordaan. Sadly, Jordaan died the following morning.

Vrolijk remembered Jordaan as being gentle and kind; a man who got on with everyone and never had a bad word to say about anybody. He was a man of culture, who never swore and who everybody liked.

5 April 1942

Barend Klooss and Hendrik Johannes 'Henk' Sebes were dropped by parachute on the evening of 5 April 1942 near the town of Ede.

Fortunately, the two men landed safely and there were no Germans waiting for them.

Klooss was born 22 October 1913 in Rotterdam. After completing his full-time education, he worked in insurance between 1934 and 1936, before then working for Diethelm & Co., a shipping and insurance company based in Saigon, until 1939.

After arriving in London, he initially enlisted in the Dutch Army before becoming a member of the SOE on 28 May 1941. During training he went by the name of Barend Kiek and was allocated the code name of 'Bob'. There are a number of reports in his SOE file, and the following was made by his instructor, Corporal Mendes, on 1 July 1941:

> Keen sense of independence, reliable. Nevertheless, he has a more cunning and shrewd character. He doesn't mind 'pose' as the French say. He is constantly asking the most ridiculous and foolish questions during lectures, which at times leaves the instructors exasperated. Difficult to tell whether he is being sincere or 'pose'. I ascribe it to the same thing all Dutchmen have in common, to look at things from a far too problematic angle making everything look far more complicated in their own minds than it is in reality.

Along with Sebes, Klooss was dropped into the Netherlands on the evening of 5 April 1942 by parachute. He was captured by the Germans on 1 May in Utrecht, and after initially spending time at Haaren, he arrived at Mauthausen on 27 November 1943, and was executed there on 6 September 1944.

Hendrik Johannes Sebes was born in Dordrecht on 23 July 1919. Having finished his full-time education in 1932, he began working as a tailor. In October 1938 he joined the Dutch Army, initially in Breda with the 6th Infantry Regiment (an anti-tank unit), until March 1939, before transferring to the 6th Frontier Battalion in Princenhage and then the 27th Infantry Regiment, in Deurne, where he remained until the outbreak of war.

Having made his way to England in January 1941, he enlisted in the SOE on 10 February. Whilst undergoing training he used the name of Henry Salberg and was given the code name of 'Lydia'. He was a quiet individual and had a pleasant personality, but was noted as being of average intelligence with an inability to be able to keep his concentration for any great period of time, hence why he was deemed not suitable for any kind of leadership, although he could be relied upon to fill a minor role.

Having been dropped into the Netherlands, along with Klooss, on the evening of 5 April 1942, Sebes managed to remain at large until 8 May, when he, too, was arrested in Rotterdam. He eventually ended up in Mauthausen, where he met his end on 7 September 1944.

18 April 1942

The next SOE agent dropped into the Netherlands was Joannes Henricus Marie 'Jan' de Haas. It was a bit of a 'hurry up' operation, as he was sent as a direct replacement for Jan Molenaar after the latter had seriously injured himself on landing, and, fearing capture and interrogation, had decided to take his own life by means of crushing a cyanide capsule in his mouth.

De Haas was born on 7 February 1918 in The Hague. His initial intention on completing his full-time secondary education was to become a priest, and to this end he became a student at the Roman Catholic College in The Hague. He enlisted in the Dutch OTC Transport Service in October 1938 and became active in the Voluntary Land Storm Corps Motor Service. In February 1941, with his country occupied by German forces, he resigned from the Dutch Army and returned to civilian life. In September 1941, a long-term friend of his, Ab Homburg, called upon him to say that he would be going to England the following March and asked if de Haas would be interested in coming with him. He also told him that he was a secret agent who worked for the SOE and had returned to the Netherlands to carry out a mission, and wanted to know if he would be able to help him.

De Haas agreed to help Homburg and the pair arranged to meet up the following week, but Homburg never showed. What de

Haas did not know was that Homburg had, in fact, been arrested by the Gestapo but had then miraculously managed to escape from Scheveningen prison. Despite the real danger they were putting themselves in, the de Haas family happily put Homburg up in their home, where he remained for a couple of weeks before being moved to another location.

On 13 February 1942, de Haas, Homburg and a friend of theirs, Jo Buizer (see entry for 22 June), a member of the Dutch resistance, arrived at IJmuiden, a coastal town on the west coast, with the intention of hiding away on board a boat and then high jacking it and making the skipper take them to England. This was never going to be easy, however, because before any Dutch fishing vessel left port, it was liable to be inspected by German military personnel to ensure that there were no stowaways on board. Miraculously, the three men boarded their chosen vessel, the *Beatrice*, and remained undiscovered when it was searched by German soldiers.

Back in IJmuiden, news spread that the *Beatrice* had been lost at sea, meaning the Germans did not carry out any reprisals against the friends and families of the ship's crew.

The *Beatrice* arrived at Yarmouth on 17 February 1942 and having already been captured by the Gestapo, it was decided that it was too much of a risk to redeploy Homburg back to the Netherlands, so he left the SOE and joined the RAF to retrain as a pilot. He was killed in action on 1 April 1945 when the aircraft he was piloting was shot down by German anti-aircraft guns at Bornebroek, near the Dutch town of Delden.

Buizer and de Haas were taken to the Royal Victorian Patriotic Society, a centre where foreign refugees were received and interviewed by members of British military intelligence to ensure they were not enemy spies attempting to gain entry to Britain. For those refugees who were purporting to be Dutch, they were further interviewed by members of the Dutch Central Intelligence Service.

De Haas was detained for three days before his interrogators were convinced by his story, after which they not only released him but let him become a member of the SOE. The usual period of time it took to fully train potential agents was six months, but de Haas, who during his training used the surname of de Heer, was deployed in under two. He was dropped off by a motor torpedo boat on the evening of 8 April 1942, off the Dutch coast at Castricum, rowing the last few hundred yards in a rubber dingy. He had been tasked with establishing a communications link between the Netherlands and Britain, and to find safe accommodation for future agents on their arrival.

On 28 April, de Haas was at home when he received a visit from Leo Andringa, an SOE agent newly arrived from Britain, and another man who was also believed to have been an agent of the SOE. Not only was the other man not an SOE operative, he was, in fact, Poos te Zijn, a member of the SD. Andringa and de Haas were immediately arrested and handed over to Joseph Schreider for interrogation. De Haas was initially transferred to a prison at Haaren on 3 August 1943, where he remained until he was transferred to Mauthausen on 27 November 1943, and executed on 7 September 1944.

29 May 1942

Hermanus Parlevliet and Toon van Steen were dropped near Kallenkote, just east of Steenwijk and were immediately arrested by the Gestapo. At least four other agents had previously landed at Kallenkote and had also immediately been arrested; a fact that neither Parlevliet or van Steen could have possibly known.

The two men had been sent to the Netherlands as a direct result of a radio message sent to the wireless set of Huub Lauwers on 1 May 1942, informing him of the time, date and location that Parlevliet and van Steen would be landing. Unfortunately for the two men, Lauwers had no way of letting London know not to send them.

They were tasked with making contact with their colleague, Leo Andringa, who had arrived in the Netherlands on the evening of 29 March. They had also been given instructions to blow up the locks of the 36-km long Juliana canal, which is located in the southern Netherlands and provides a bypass of the River Meuse between Maastricht and Maasbracht, and which was seen as important shipping link between Germany and Belgium. They were also tasked with looking into the viability of opening up a new sea route for the delivery and ex-filtration of future agents, as well as to carry out acts of sabotage against nominated railway targets, along with ad-hoc acts of sabotage, as and when opportunities arose.

Hermanus Parlevliet was born in the town of Baarle Nassau on 16 May 1916. In October 1936, aged 20, he enlisted in the Dutch Army to complete his mandatory national service. He later went on to serve as non-commissioned officer in the Dutch mounted police from early 1938. He initially spent six months undergoing his training at Apeldoorn, with his first station being with the Asten Brigade in Brabant, before he was then redeployed to another detachment for nineteen months.

The war was into its fourth year before Parlevliet managed to make his way across the North Sea to England, eventually becoming an SOE agent on 22 February 1942.

During his training, Parlevliet used the name of Herman Pijnakker, and as agent in the field used the alias Herman Prins. His operational code name was 'Pute'.

Parlevliet eventually became a prisoner at Rawicz prison, and as with other captured SOE and MI6 agents, it is not known for certain where or when he met his fate, but his official death has been recorded as 30 April 1944.

Parlevliet is a particularly interesting case because the Dutch section of the SOE had records which stated that his arrest was confirmed by a German document dated 24 June 1942. It did not, however, confirm what that document was, or when the SOE first became aware of its existence. The point that needs to be raised here is that after 24 June 1942, thirty more Dutch agents were dropped into the Netherlands. All of these agents were immediately arrested upon landing. Knowing when the SOE became aware of the German document in question becomes all the more important when trying to identify what and when the SOE actually did or did not know about their agents' fates once they had been dropped behind enemy lines.

The SOE knew at this time that Parleviet was a prisoner of the Germans, but what they did not know was where he was being held, although they had managed to narrow this down to either Hertogen-Bosch prison, located in the Dutch province of North Brabant, or Scheveningen, north-west of The Hague.

Parlevliet was also somewhat different because of his unusual appearance. He was nearly 6 feet 3 inches, had a noticeably long face, and black curly hair, which it could be argued did not make him an ideal candidate to be able to function effectively as an agent as he would certainly stand out of the crowd; drawing attention to oneself was not high on the list of useful traits for an agent.

At the end of his training, he received the following comments and observations from Lieutenant Colonel Richard Thornton Hewitt, the man in charge of SOE training, in relation to the different disciplines he had received training in.

> **Demolitions:** Good.
> **Signalling:** Average.
> **Map Reading:** Good progress. Has worked hard.
> **Physical Training:** Good. Fit.
> **Fieldcraft:** Shows initiative. Good. Thorough. Shows initiative.
> **Explosives:** Good. Has progressed well.
> **Communications:** Good. Greatly improved.
> **General Remarks:** A reliable man. He has worked hard throughout the course. He is an efficient man with more brain than he appeared to have at first. He is in fact a good all-round man and reliable. Should prove useful.

The same SOE file also included the following from the same commanding officer: 'Not brilliant but sound, observant and self-reliant. Has plenty of common sense. A quiet but reliable character who should prove a useful assistant who it is believed would be suitable for deployment as an agent.'

The latter of the two comments was perhaps made earlier in the course, which would possibly explain the minor differences between the two.

One of the SOE's instructors, Sergeant Webb, wrote the following brief report about Parlevliet on 19 June 1941: 'A very quiet, well-educated man, intelligent to a degree and very interested in the different aspects of the course. A very promising pupil. He is a regular soldier.'

The other agent who landed with Parleviet, Toon van Steen, was born on 5 December 1912 in the Dutch town of Ubbergen. He enlisted in the SOE on 22 February 1942 and during his training used the alias of van Sittard. An early report about him included the following description: 'A quiet man. Not outstandingly good in any subject. Very slow but thorough and reliable. Difficult to classify.' Clearly, he did not create an immediately positive impression in the minds of his instructors. The report continued:

Has had about 10 years' service in the Marechaussee, Dutch Mounted Police. Before that he was a quarry worker near Ubbergen between 1926 and 1932. He has also had to do with light locomotives and is very interested in them and in their destruction. He is showing keenness and promise in demolitions. He is a very quiet and methodical man, who was not well understood at first. He has been much less retiring since his conversation with N and is doing good work.

Van Steen was certainly not an individual considered for a leadership role. In fact, there is a particular paragraph included in his file, with no date or author against it, which brings into question his suitability to have even been considered as an effective agent with the SOE: 'Dull and unintelligent. He has done his best but has failed to grasp the course and cannot be recommended for any category.'

It is quite remarkable for such negative comments to have been written about van Steen, and for him to have then been deemed suitable for deployment on an active operation just a matter of weeks later.

After his arrest, and having initially been interrogated at the local police station at Steenwijk, van Steen arrived at Haaren on 31 May 1942, where he remained until 27 November 1943, when he was moved to Mauthausen. He was shot by German guards on 31 December 1944, some eight months after Parlevliet had met his death.

Like a number of his SOE colleagues, he was posthumously awarded the Bronze Cross by the Dutch government on 2 May 1953.

22 June 1942

Jan Jacob van Rietschoten and Johannis (Jo) Jan Cornelis Buizer were dropped near the Dutch village of Holten on the evening of 22 June 1942. Unfortunately for the two men, their reception committee was not a group from the local resistance movement, but members of the local Gestapo. They were then taken to the POW camp at Haaren, where they were interrogated by the SD. Van Rietschoten and two other prisoners, Arie Cornelis van der Giessen and Antonius Johannes Wegner, managed to escape from the camp on 21 November. The three men managed to stay at large for some time, but Wegner was the first to be re-captured in January 1944 whilst making his way into Spain via the Pyrenees. Meanwhile, van der Giessen and van Rietschoten were both arrested at Roosendaal on 5 May 1944, enroute to Belgium. It is quite possible that the pair were doubled crossed by known double agent Christiaan Lindemans. They were taken back to Haaren, where they remained until 27 November 1943, before being moved onto Mauthausen, where they were shot and killed by firing squad on 10 June 1944.

Van Rietschoten was born on 25 August 1921 in Rotterdam. During his SOE training he used the alias of Jan van Rossum, and once operational he also used the alias of Johan van Rooyen. His code name was 'Jan'.

At the outbreak of the war, the 18-year-old van Rietschoten was a student in Delft, but had no intention of just sitting out the war in relative comfort as a civilian. On the night of 24 September 1941, along with his three friends Armand Maassen, Dolf Scherpbier and Wim Helibron, the four men climbed into two folding canoes, with Rietschoten and Maassen in one and Scherpbier and Helibron in the other. They set sail from Katwijk but Scherpbier and Helibron's journey did not last long. After rowing for only a matter of yards, their canoe began to sink so they abandoned their attempt and returned to the beach. As for Rietschoten and Maassen, exhausted, wet and hungry, they made it to England, arriving there on 27 September. He joined the SOE on 15 October and was given the courtesy rank of 2nd Lieutenant.

Van Rietschoten's SOE file contains a note dated 15 October 1941 that says: 'Jan Jacob van Rietschoten is being taken over from the Dutch authorities today for training as a prospective agent. Registered as a civilian alien in the above name. For training purposes, he will be known as John van Rossem.'

Just because an individual was considered to be a suitable candidate to commence training as an agent for the SOE, MI6, or another branch of military intelligence, this did not always mean they would complete the course to the required standard. If a student failed, or the instructors deemed they were unsuitable, for security reasons, the decision might be taken to incarcerate them for as long as was deemed necessary. If this occurred, it could have dire consequences for the individual concerned.

Van Rietschoten's last training location was at STS 31, in Beaulieu, Hampshire. His final report from his time there, read as follows:

Intelligent, hardworking and enthusiastic. He has some practical ability and initiative. He is, however, so young that he is liable to be easily influenced by others older than himself and on this account is hardly suitable as a leader. Has a very pleasant but not outstanding personality. Is very modest and inspires less confidence than he deserved.

The reference to him being 'so young' was because at the time of this particular course, van Rietschoten was still only 20 years of age.

As for Jo Buizer, he was born on 11 September 1918 in the village of Almkerk. It was there that he attended elementary school, but by the time he reached secondary school age, the family had moved to Rotterdam. When he was 17 years old, he started working as an office clerk, and from there he went to work at the Dutch Post and Telegraph Service, where he became a wireless operator.

In March 1938 he began his compulsory one year's military service with the 22nd Regiment of Infantry. By the time he finished he had reached the rank of Sergeant. Just five months later, on 29 August 1939 Buizer was mobilised and transferred to the Engineers. During the German invasion of the Netherlands he was stationed at the wireless station at Voorberg, before being demobilised on 14 February 1940, when he returned to his civilian job in Amsterdam as a wireless operator. During this time Buizer was ordered by the Germans to monitor African, American and British wireless stations.

He eventually managed to escape from the Netherlands with a few of his friends on board the Dutch trawler *Beatrice* and made his way to England, where he arrived at Great Yarmouth on 17 February 1942 and was recruited by the SOE on 10 March. During his three months of training, much of which took place in the wilds of Scotland, he used the surname of Brouwers, and as agent in the field he also used the aliases of Buzzard or Burgman. In keeping with the vegetable theme of code names given to SOE agents who became involved in Operation North Pole, Buizer was allocated that of 'Spinach'.

It was clear from the SOE's own records on Buizer that they were not aware of where and when he was arrested, as his file showed that he was 'arrested 1942/43, Rawicz, Poland', although it is questionable as to whether he was ever held at Rawicz prison. The origin of this report was from an unnamed SOE agent, who claimed to have seen him there in July 1944.

In Bruizer's file held at The National Archives is a one-page document which all SOE agents had to sign in relation to the work that they did and for the organisation they worked for:

DECLARATION
I declare that I will never disclose to anyone any information which I have acquired or may at any future time acquire as the result of my connection with this department, unless such disclosure is necessary for my work for the Department. In particular I declare that except under the conditions aforementioned, I will in no circumstances give away any information concerning:-
(1). The name, alias, description, identity, location or duties of any past, present or future members of this Department.
(2). The name, aliases description, identity, location or duties of any member of staff, or any person working with this Department either as a member of the forces or as a civilian.
(3). The nature, methods, objects or subjects of instruction of this Department.

(4). The location or name of any establishment of this Department.

(5). The past, present or future location, movement or employment, either potential or factual, of myself, any other member of or any person working for this Department.

I declare moreover that I understand that I am personally responsible for any disclosure of such information I may make and that disciplinary proceedings under the Official Secrets Act 1911 and 1920, the Treachery Act 1940, or the Defence (General) Regulations 1939 may be taken against me if I at any time or in any way contravene the terms of this declaration.

The document is dated 13 May 1942; the very date Buizer became a member of the SOE. Soon after landing near Holten, Rietschoten and Buizer were arrested by waiting German forces and taken to the SD prison at Haaren for interrogation. The two men had been tasked with training members of the local resistance movement to be able to carry out acts of sabotage. Not much else is known about what happened to Buizer, or where he was held, until he was eventually murdered at Mauthausen on 6 September 1944, although it is believed he had been held there for some months.

26 June 1942

Georges Louis Jambroes and Josef Bukkens were dropped into the Netherlands on 26 June as part of operation Marrow II (Major), but at the different location of Kallenkote. They were both arrested soon after they landed. One of those present when they were arrested was one of the Netherlands' most infamous collaborators of the Second World War, Anton van der Waals.

Jambroes was born on 22 May 1905 in Amsterdam. After leaving school he went to work at the Philips bulb factory in Eindhoven as an assistant in the laboratory and was also working for Batappsche Petroleum company in Amsterdam, carrying out research for three and a half years. Alongside his work, he also continued his studies and went on to obtain a degree in mathematics. In 1934 he began working as a maths teacher in Zaandam and continued to do so until March 1941.

Jambroes had first seen military service when he was called up in 1924 and was sent to 'Officers' School' in Utrecht. In January 1929 he was promoted to the rank of Lieutenant as a reserve in the Mechanised Regiment Haarden. At the outbreak of war he served with the 15th Artillery Regiment, but was discharged in July 1941 and resumed teaching.

Politically, he was a member of the Social Democratic Labour Party until 1934, but with the rise of the Nazi Party in Germany showing National Socialism in its true colours, Jambroes became one of its strongest opponents, passionately disliking everything that it stood for.

In 1940 he became a member of the Order Service, which up until 1942 was the largest, secret anti-German organisation in the Netherlands. In February 1941, he became involved in the country's general strike, an action which saw him obliged to resign his teaching position. On 16 March 1941 he received a warning from a couple of his friends that he was been watched very closely by the Gestapo. With his name and description known to the Germans, he decided that it was best to go into hiding, staying with a number of different families at different locations across the country.

Having finally left the Netherlands on 14 October 1941, he made his way to England via Geneva, Switzerland and Portugal, arriving on 25 March 1942, when he was then interrogated by a member of British military intelligence. With his interrogators happy that he was not a German spy, he was allowed to enlist in the SOE, which he did on 23 May. Whilst undertaking his training, he used the alias of Gerard Lodewijk Jurgens. Once an active agent in the field, he also used the surnames of Jansen, Johannes and Jonkers. When using the latter of the three, he used the Christian names Gerrit Leendert.

Jambroes' case was different because despite the usual six months it took to train an agent, the period of time between his enlistment and his capture by the Germans was just thirty-five days. One of the tasks he was given upon landing in the Netherlands was to contact the one of the three main Dutch resistance groups called the 'Order Service' or the OD group, which he had previously been part of, but instead he was immediately arrested. The day after his capture he was imprisoned at Haaren, where he remained until 27 November 1943 before being moved to Mauthausen, where he was murdered on 7 September 1944. On 2 May 1953 he was posthumously awarded the Dutch Bronze Cross, the citation of which read as follows: 'He has distinguished himself as a member of a secret intelligence agency that has dispatched him in the years between 1940 and 1945 to enemy held territory where he had to perform life threatening actions under extremely trying circumstances that ultimately led to his death by enemy counteraction.'

The citation is inaccurate, however, as Jambroes was arrested as soon as he landed in the Netherlands, meaning he did not have the opportunity to perform any actions at all.

Josef Bukkens was born in Vlissingen on 8 June 1916. He escaped to England on board the Dutch vessel *Batavier II*, which sailed out of Cherbourg, France and arrived in England on 31 May 1940. Prior to his escape, he had been a Lieutenant in the Dutch Air Force.

He enlisted in the SOE on 23 May 1942, and, like his compatriot Jambroes, was captured on 27 June 1942, just thirty-five days after his training had begun. During his training, he had used the surname of Boogard and once in the field he used the alias of Evert Loonhuizen.

He, too, was initially incarcerated at Haaren and was then transferred to Mauthausen on 27 November 1943, before being murdered there on 7 September 1944.

23 July 1942

Gerard John 'Heck Blue' van Hemert was, in fact, American, being born on 28 April 1920 in Brooklyn, New York, after his parents had emigrated there with their two daughters and another son. However, just a few years after van Hemert's birth, the family returned to live in the Netherlands.

Soon after turning 21, he returned to the United States and found work in New York at the recruitment office of the Dutch armed forces. Rather than enlist in either the US or Dutch military, he chose instead to make his way to England and join the British

Intelligence Service. Despite being American by birth and spending a number of years living in the Netherlands, he arrived in England on a British passport in December 1941. He enlisted in the SOE on 15 January 1942 and during his training used the aliases of Gerrit van Haaften and Gerrit van Hemert, with the code name of 'Jacob'.

The SOE file on van Hemert includes an unauthored report about him dated 25 May 1942, just two months before he was dropped into the Netherlands:

> A certain Colonel van Sas, late military Attaché for the Dutch in Berlin, has acted as one of our contacts in America in the past. Colonel van Sas went to America (Date unknown) on a sort of Dutch Military Mission, presumably when Holland fell, and came to England about four weeks ago. Whilst he was in the USA he recruited for us van Haaften [van Hemert], who is an American citizen but had lived most of his life in Holland. Van Haaften managed to get an exit permit from Holland just before the USA declared war. He is now in training at STS 53 and is nearly ready for the 'off'.
>
> The present story goes than van Sas and van Haaften met, possibly over the weekend of 25-26 April in London when van Haaften was on leave at the Park View Hotel. After this meeting a second one took place at a hotel outside London during the weekend of 9-10 May. Again, van Haaften was on leave in London at that time and was staying once more at the Park View Hotel. Three others were present. At this meeting certain projects were discussed and van Sas suggested that van Haaften should do some special task for him in Holland. Van Haaften has not given the names of the persons present or the addresses at which these meetings took place, but he has refused to give any details concerning the conversation or the projects. This information was obtained from van Haaften on 23rd May.
>
> The background of this 'intrigue', which appears to be going on behind our back, may well be that van Sas is a supporter of van Sandt, who is thought to be in political conflict with our Dutch opposite numbers. NO would like a special

enquiry made concerning van Sas, but no mention should be made of the fact that he has been contacted and appears to be having dealings with one of our men. There may be a possibility that van Sas may be indulging in double-dealing.

The van Sas referred to in the notes was Colonel Bert Sas, who was the Netherlands' military attaché in Berlin at the time of the German invasion in May 1940. Over the years he had spent working in Germany he had built an excellent working relationship with Colonel Hans Oster, an officer with the German Abwehr. Their relationship was such that Oster, no lover of Hitler and the Nazis, had, in August 1939, informed Sas of the impending German invasion of Poland. Consequently, the only nation to mobilise their forces was the Netherlands. Oster later advised Sas of Germany's impending invasion of the Netherlands, Belgium and France, but despite him passing this information to his 'superiors', it was not taken seriously until it was too late.

It is strange that the report on van Hemert's file included the belief that van Sas might well be a double-agent, which means by association the same suspicion could just as well be aimed at van Hemert. But despite these real concerns, the SOE was still prepared to send him out on his mission to the Netherlands.

He was dropped on the night of 23 July 1942 near the village of Holten and immediately arrested by the Gestapo. He was initially detained at Haaren before being moved to Mauthausen on 27 November 1943, and executed on 7 September 1944. At the time of his death, he was just 24 years of age.

Van Hemert was posthumously awarded the Bronze Cross on 2 May 1953, and the War Commemorative Cross on 24 June 1953.

24 September 1942

For some unknown reason, no SOE agents were dropped into the Netherlands during August 1942. The following month, however, four SOE agents, Karel Willem Adriaan Beukema toe Water, Cornelis 'Kees' Droogleever Fortuyn, Adriaan Klaas Mooy, and Roelof Christiaan Jongelie, were dropped near Rijssen on the night of 24 September, but were captured by the Germans immediately upon landing. The following day they were taken to the prison camp at Haaren, where they remained for more than a year before being moved to Mauthausen, where they were killed on 7 September 1944. The file on the four men also states that they were seen at the Rawicz prison camp in July 1944. The individual who had supposedly seen the men was an escaped French agent, but there was no explanation on the file as to how this agent recognised them, presumably having never seen them before. In the circumstances, it is highly unlikely that the four Dutchmen would have betrayed their true identities and what they had been up to before their arrest.

Karel Willem Adriaan Beukema toe Water was born on 20 June 1909, in Tegal, Indonesia. After finishing his education, he qualified as a chemical engineer and became a Lieutenant in the Dutch Army Reserve.

Having made his way to England, he enlisted in the SOE on 18 June 1942, and used the surname of Beekman whilst undergoing his training at STS 6, in Wokingham, Berkshire. His SOE file contains a number of brief reports about how he progressed throughout the course:

2 July 1942 – Lance Corporals Boks and Mendes
A conscientious student, assimilating thoroughly and easily everything taught here, although appearing to know quite a lot about it already. Very fond of physical exercise; his chief hobby being mountaineering. Maintains a very friendly and unassuming attitude towards the men from the other ranks without becoming on the other hand, too familiar.

By August he had moved on to STS 24, at Inverie House, at Knoydart in Invernesshire. His report there was even more glowing in its praise:

3 August 1942 – Unnamed Instructor and Commandant
Throughout the course this officer has worked hard and reached a good standard in all subjects, particularly demolitions and weapon training. I am grateful for the help he has given me on this course. He has spent much of his time assisting

students with their revision and preparations for schemes and untiring keenness and energy have been invaluable.

He is an outstanding student. Intelligent, courageous and sufficiently ruthless. He is an excellent organiser and instructor. On schemes, his planning has been thorough and his action decisive. A strong character.

Included in his SOE file is a seven-page report dated 6 August 1943, entitled 'Crossed Lines in Holland'. It also contains a further ten pages of appendices. The report is far too large to replicate in the pages of this book, but in essence it appears to be a discussion about concerns as to whether radio transmissions being received from the Netherlands were actually from British and Dutch agents under the control of the Abwehr, or agents of the latter masquerading as Allied agents.

On 21 July 1943, a message was received by the SIS in London which was alleged to have come from Switzerland and read as follows: 'Reliable source recently arrived from Holland states on March 9th, 8 parachutists, including a woman came down in Holland but were immediately captured by the enemy and put into prison at HAREN. One of these gave away source and password which is, "I am friend of MARIUS".'

There were, however, errors with this message. Haren is spelt incorrectly (it should be Haaren) and while the password quoted was correct, on 9 March 1943 there were only three SOE agents dropped into Holland, and there is no explanation as to why this particular report is attached to Beukema toe Water's SOE file.

Cornelis Droogleever Fortuyn was born in Amsterdam on 10 April 1922. In his teenage years he went to study at the university in Leiden, but by July 1940, a number of the university's students had fled the Netherlands for the sanctuary and relative safety of England. But it was no easy journey. Along with a friend, Louis d'Aulnis, Droogleever Fortuyn decided to do the same and the two men took what was known as the Van Niftrik escape route, named after a Dutch reserve Army officer and his wife Elisabeth.

The route started in the Dutch border village of Putte, with the first stage of it taking escapees to Antwerp, a distance of just over 22 miles. From there the route took them on to France and required them to take a train from Paris to Toulouse. During that particular stage of the journey, the two men were asked by a German guard where their final destination was and the reason for their journey. D'Aulnis spotted that the guard was wearing a medal on his uniform indicating he had served his country during the First World War and engaged him in conversation about it. The guard, clearly an astute individual, looked back at D'Aulnis and said, 'I will only arrest you when we arrive in Toulouse', then turned and walked away. This gesture allowed the pair to safely get off the train at Lyon.

The men subsequently made their way into Spain across the Pyrenees but were arrested soon after their arrival and incarcerated in the Castillo de Figueras, in Cervera, Catalonia. From there they were transferred to a Spanish concentration camp at Miranda de Ebro, but after just a couple of months a group of men from the camp, including D'Aulis and Droogleever Fortuyn, were allowed to leave and travel by train to Madrid, where they were taken to the Dutch Embassy and freedom. But their journey to England was far from over. Having waited for more than five months for a visa to leave the country, they finally left the Spanish capital on 12 December 1941 and made the 330-mile journey to Seville. It was on Boxing Day 1941 that the two men boarded the Polish passenger ship, the *Batory*, to Gibraltar, before arriving in Glasgow on 4 January 1942. When they arrived in London, they were interrogated by members of the British Intelligence Service, after which time they were recruited and became part of the SOE on 24 March 1942.

By the time Droogleever Fortuyn began his course he had only just turned 20 years of age, and although his training reports were all above average, the point which was mentioned time and time again was his age. Although it was recognised he was intelligent, well-educated, a hard worker, and quick to pick things up, he was considered to be too young to be a leader because it was believed he would struggle to handle older and more experienced men, and thus lead to him being vague and indecisive in his instruction and decision-making.

Adriaan Klaas Mooy was born in Amersfort on 11 July 1919, the son of Anton Jacobus Cornelis Mooy, a well-known organist and composer. After finishing school in 1936 he attended the Royal

Marine college at Den Helder, where he remained until February 1938 when he decided to leave as he was not enjoying his time as a student. After having time to reflect on his decision, he changed his mind and seven months later, in September 1938, he became a student at the Military College at Breda, with a view to becoming an officer in the artillery of the Indian Army. After the Netherlands was invaded in May 1940, he was discharged from his academy training on 15 July, but remained attached to the labour corps until 16 September, when he was fully discharged from military service and sent home.

The following information is taken from an SOE report concerning the interrogation of Mooy after he arrived in Britain in April 1942. It was carried out by a member of British military intelligence and the report is dated 16 April 1942. The interrogation shows that nationals of European countries under German occupation arriving in Britain during the war were not immediately welcomed with 'open arms' or accepted at 'face value'. They were interrogated in minute detail to establish the truth, as far as it was possible to do so, as to why they had made the journey. It would not have been beyond the realms of possibility that the German Abwehr would have sent any number of their agents to Britain, masquerading as refugees.

On 19 October 1941, Mooy began his journey to Britain by making his way to Breda by train with two of his friends, the Blom brothers. When they arrived at their destination, they flagged down a taxi and asked the driver to take them to the Dutch-Belgian border. After being dropped off, the three men began looking for a convenient location where they could safely cross. After having walked for only a matter of minutes, they heard footsteps and quickly dived to the ground, fearing the worst. It was so dark that the men responsible for the footsteps actually tripped over Mooy and the Blom brothers. Fortunately, rather than being members of the Gestapo or a German army unit, it was a couple of Belgian smugglers who helped them to safely cross the border into Belgium. From there they caught a tram into Antwerp where the three men stayed with a relative of the Bloms. Although one of the Blom brothers decided to return to the Netherlands after about a week, Mooy and Karel Blom continued on to Brussels, and from there to Mons, where they spent a night at a small hotel. After a much-needed good night's sleep, the pair set off for the town of Tournay. From here they walked across country, a distance of nearly 17 miles, to the French city of Lille, without coming into contact with either Belgian or French police, or any German soldiers.

From Lille they caught the train to Albert and from there walked the relatively short distance to Corbie, where during the hours of darkness they decided to swim across the River Somme, removing their clothes and tying them the best they could in a bundle above their heads. On reaching the opposite side of the river they found themselves in Aubigny, where they made their way to the nearest farm. The family who lived there were Flemish speaking and both the farmer and his family were kind, friendly and helpful towards Mooy and Blom, providing them with a hearty meal and allowing them to stay overnight whilst their clothes dried.

The next morning the two men left by train from the nearby town of Villers Bretonneux and made their way to Amiens, where they changed and continued by an express train back to Lille and then on to Paris, where they stayed with an uncle of Karel Blom for two days. Mooy and Blom, in company with the latter's uncle, then caught a train to Vierzon, where they changed trains and continued on to Bléré la Croix. On arrival the three men met a 'passeur' or smuggler, a woman in her mid-twenties, in a small café opposite the train station. After they had chatted for a while and everybody accepted, they were not been led into some kind of a trap, Blom's uncle returned to Paris, whilst Mooy and Blom set off for the town of Francueil, where they then caught a bus to Chateauroux. Once there they caught a train to Toulouse. However, they arrived too late to go to the Office Neerlandais, and instead spent the night sleeping in the local cemetery. The next morning, they returned to the office, from where they were taken to the Dutch refugee camp at La Fourgette. A few days later all those in the camp of military age were transferred to the French camp at Clerfond, with a view to them being put to work.

On arriving at the camp, it quickly became clear to Mooy that he was not going to receive the kind of assistance he was looking for to help get him to England. With the option of trying to cross the

Pyrenees out of the question due to heavy snow, he decided instead that his best option was to return to Karel Blom's uncle's home on the outskirts of Paris.

A few days later, Mooy arrived back in Paris. Blom's uncle was surprised to see him, especially as his nephew, Karel, was not with him, having decided to remain at the refugee camp at Clerfond. These were times of war, of mistrust and betrayal so regardless of whether or not Mr Blom believed what Mooy was saying, he had no way of checking the validity of what he was being told.

Over the next week or so Mooy continued his journey on foot, by bus and train and with the help of a number of individuals as he travelled through France, Belgium and Holland, before finally reaching neutral Switzerland in the back of a cart, where he was immediately arrested by the local Swiss police and taken to the nearby town of Neuchatel. He was kept in prison there for four days, uncertain as to what fate held in store for him, before being transferred to the Dutch Legation in Bern, where he was interrogated by the legation's General van Tright. Happy with Mooy's story, van Tright sent him to the Hotel du Lac, situated on the outskirts of Geneva, where he sat and waited for more than three months.

The relevant documentation, visas and a passport were eventually obtained for Mooy to leave for Curacao in the Dutch East Indies, via Brazil. Having left Bern by train on 26 March 1942, he arrived in Madrid after changing trains in Barcelona, eventually arriving in Lisbon on 31 March, where he met with Dutch Consul officials who in turn took him to the British Consulate, where he was provided with a visa for entry into the United Kingdom, where he arrived on 9 April.

Mooy's interrogator would have repeated the questions more than once to see if his story changed at all. He would have wanted the names of any individuals who were referred to and the addresses of any locations he had visited. It was crucial that the interrogators were thorough with their questioning, because if they got it wrong, a German agent may have ended up working for British Intelligence.

The report ended with the following conclusion:

During his journey to Switzerland, Mooy appears to have been very fortunate in not being 'controlled' anywhere. He makes a very good and frank impression, however, and I do not think there is any reason to doubt his integrity.

From Switzerland he has been passed on to this country with a false passport in the usual manner, and I recommend that he should be released to the Dutch authorities.

I believe the comment in the first paragraph of the conclusion about 'not being controlled' is a reference to the fact that at no time during his journey was he stopped, detained or suspected of any wrongdoing by German or other national authorities.

Mooy became a member of the SOE on 20 May 1942, just five weeks after he had been interrogated after his arrival in Britain. The following are remarks made on Mooy's file by one of his instructors and the Commandant of the training facility where Mooy's undertook his training.

9 June 1942 – Unnamed Instructor's Remarks
An intelligent student. He has mastered all subjects with ease but has lately been handicapped by a sprained arm.

23 September 1942 – Commandant's Report
Had no previous mechanical or industrial experience but was an intelligent and interested student who acquired a fair grasp of all the lectures he attended. Demolition work moderate. Shows organising ability, but he is inclined to be self-centred and moody. He would have done better if he could have remained until the end of the course.

The Commandant's report is interesting for two reasons. Firstly, because it is dated the day before Mooy was dropped into the Netherlands, and secondly because it was deemed necessary for Mooy to become an active agent and sent on his mission to the Netherlands before having actually completed his course, when there must have been other SOE agents who had completed their training and were sitting round waiting to be deployed.

A file held on Mooy by the SOE recorded that information had been received in June 1943 saying he had been seen by two unnamed

SOE agents as a prisoner at Haaren concentration camp. The two agents managed to escape from the same camp in August 1943 and make their way back to Britain, arriving in November 1943. The two men referred to are believed to be the SOE agents Dourlein and Ubbink. Subsequent to his capture and interrogation, Mooy eventually ended up in a prison camp in Rawicz, where he was likely murdered on 30 April 1944.

On 2 May 1953 he was posthumously awarded the Bronze Cross, the citation of which read as follows, the last line of which being a rather unusual way of saying he was murdered by the Germans whilst in captivity: 'Distinguished himself by courageous action against the enemy as an agent of a secret intelligence service, which during the years 1940-1945 sent him to enemy occupied territory, where he had a life threatening task to perform under extremely difficult circumstances, which eventually led to his death through enemy counteraction.'

Roelof Christiaan Jongelie was born on 25 February 1903 in Amsterdam. As a teenager he had attended Nautical School in Amsterdam, before joining the Mercantile Marine and attending the Wireless School in Amsterdam. In 1924 he joined the Royal Netherlands Navy as an officer in the Naval Reserve. Between 1926 and the outbreak of the war in 1939, he had worked as a Port Officer in Surabaya, the Dutch East Indies.

He was mobilised on 29 August 1939 and saw military action in the Dutch East Indies from 1941 to 1942, and on 3 March 1942, just six days before the Dutch surrender to the Japanese, he was evacuated from Java and sailed on a number of ships via Colombo and South Africa, before arriving in England on 2 May 1942, where he was initially employed at the Royal Netherlands Naval Headquarters in London. On 3 July, he began his training to become an SOE agent. His code name was 'Arie' and he was part of Operation Parsley. His name during his training to become an SOE agent was Loek Jansma and once operational in the field, he used the name of Henri Jean Cornielle Haver.

His SOE file is rather brief, and the lack of comments or observations made by any members of the training team are noticeable. The only note on his file, dated 14 October 1942, was

'From: NO' to 'D/CE.3' stating the following: 'JANSMA, I regret to inform you that news has been received to the effect that this agent, who left for the field on the night of the 24/25 September, is dead.'

The day after his arrest Jongelie was held in captivity at Haaren. He was seen alive and well at the Rawicz camp in July 1944, and is known to have arrived at Mauthausen sometime after that, before being murdered there on 7 September 1944. This obviously leads to the conclusion that the note on his file dated 14 October 1942, is incorrect.

1 October 1942

Arie Cornelis van der Giessen was born on 2 August 1916 in Krimpen aan den IJssel, and before the outbreak of the war had worked at his father's shipyard located in their hometown.

His SOE file includes a letter sent by the then head of Section N Major Richard Laming to Lieutenant Colonel Cuthbert Rabagliati, an officer serving with the Secret Intelligence Service (MI6). Rabagliati, working with François van 't Sant, head of the Dutch Central Intelligence Department in London, was responsible for the infiltration of a number of SOE/MI6 agents into the Netherlands. The letter is dated 29 October 1941.

Dear Rabagliati,

Arie Cornelis Van Der Giessen
As you know, the Netherlands Government released J.J. van Rietschoten for service with this section. He has a friend who has arrived in England with whom I have been in contact, and who has expressed a wish to join us. He is Arie Cornelis van der Giessen, born 2nd August 1916 at Krimpen aan den IJssel, Sergeant for special services Royal Netherlands Navy, temporary address: Bangor Hotel, Bedford Place, WC1. The special services referred to are those of ship-building and repairing. He was for some time employed at Southampton, but his work there has ceased, and I understand he is more or less at a loose end as he failed to pass the examination for

a commission in the Royal Netherlands Navy. He is a well-known sailing man and has got guts.

I should be greatly obliged if you would officially apply for van der Giessen's release. In the circumstances I doubt there will be much objection. I should be very grateful if you would let me know as soon as possible, so that I may train two friends in work for which they are quite obviously suited.

During his SOE training, van der Giessen used the names of Arie van Krimpen and once in the field he used the alias Anton Gerrit Groen. He was dropped into the Netherlands late in the evening of 1 October 1942, for what was known as Operation Cabbage, and was allocated the code name of 'Bram'. On landing he was immediately arrested by the Germans, who were awaiting his arrival.

In November 1943, two SOE agents who had been held captive by the Germans at Haaren, arrived back in Britain after having escaped from the camp three months earlier. They confirmed a report which had reached the SOE in June 1943 that van der Giessen had been captured and held at the same camp. What the file did not include was the name of the two agents who managed to escape from Haaren, although the men in question were Johan Bernard Ubbink and Pieter Dourlein.

The official SOE file on van der Giessen states that in December 1944, they received an intelligence report from a trusted source stating that 'van der Giessen had escaped from the camp at Haaren on or around 28 November 1944, but they did not know his present where abouts.'

Another two-page document in the same SOE file, which also mentions van der Giessen, is a good example of wartime confusion and contradiction, especially in the world of espionage and military intelligence. The document is not dated or signed, but references it contains indicate it must have been compiled sometime after March 1945: 'You will recollect that Jan Jacob van Rietschoten [code name 'Jay-Jay'] (PARSNIP)] and Aat van der GIESSEN [code name 'Bram'] (CABBAGE) were reported as having escaped from Haaren in about November, 1943, which was after the escape of CHIVE and SPROUT.'

'Parsnip' and 'Cabbage' were the operations that van Rietschoten and van der Giessen were deployed on, while 'CHIVE' and 'SPROUT' refer to Johan Bernhard Ubbink and Pieter Dourlein. Ubbink had been dropped into the Netherlands on the evening of 29 November 1942, and was immediately captured. Dourlein followed on the night of 9/10 March 1943 and was also immediately captured by the Germans (see 29 November 1942).

So far as the Special Section has been informed, the story of those agents is that in November 1943, we received information that PARSNIP and CABBAGE together with a third agent, Wegener (LACROSSE), had been successful in escaping, since when nothing further has been heard of PARSNIP and CABBAGE.

WEGENER did however manage to reach Belgium where he contacted an SIS agent who transmitted a message on his behalf asking what he should do; when SIS sent the reply, which they had agreed with N Section, their agent was so frightened of his contact that he refused to have anything more to do with WEGENER, who also therefore faded from the picture.

Most recently a Mr C DROOGLEEVER FORTUYN of Room 736 Arlington House, Arlington Street, SW1, has written on 29th March, 1945 to General J.W. Van Oorschot at Hereford House to state that his brother, who lives in Maastricht, was actually contacted by WEGENER in the period between his escape from Haaren and his arrival in Belgium. It appears that he told DROOGLEEVER FORTUYN in Maastricht the story of what had happened, but this man took fright and he thought he was an agent provocateur and did, in fact, nothing whatever to help him. He has since been shown a photograph of WEGENER and has recognised it as his unwelcome caller. Both were the sons of wealthy fathers and it was always thought that they must have gone under-ground and been maintained in hiding by their families, though from the information at our disposal this does not now seem to have been the case.

Since N Section have been unable to trace these agents since the liberation of Holland and in view of the fact that they have not contacted their families, one must suppose that they met with some mischance after their escape and been deported to Germany or executed.

We have now received further information as follows:-

J.J. Rietschoten crossed in September 1941, by canoe from Holland to England. He was dropped as parachutist over Holland in May 1942, and was almost immediately taken by the Germans and put in a prison at Haaren (North Brabant). After about one year A. van der Giesen was also dropped as a parachutist, taken prisoner and joined V Rietschoten at Haaren prison. About half a year later both boys escaped from Haaren prison and went to Rotterdam where they were hiding. They were able to contact their parents through the intermediary of a well trusted friend of the family.

At the beginning of May 1944, they departed somehow for Bergen op Zoom, and it is known that they arrived there. Then they crossed from Bergen op Zoom to South Beveland with the intention to cross back to England. So far, no reliable confirmation of this has come to hand. No one has ever received their secret code-word of safe arrival.

On 25th May 1944, news came from Geneva, a postcard, for the parents of van der Giessen, that he was well and hoped soon to write a letter. This was accepted in Holland as proof that they had both arrived safely in England. No news from J.J. van Rietschoten. In March 1945, news came through a girlfriend that J.J. van Rietschoten had been seen by someone in London. The person whom had seen him was also dropped by parachute in September near Amsterdam. He told this girlfriend a story in September, of two boys who had escaped Haaren prison. When asked if he knew the boys, he replied yes, and that he had seen one of the boys in July 1944 in London.

Steps have been taken to locate this person and to check this information. There is also news that J.J. van Rietschoten was alright in December 1944, and was seen in England in

February 1945. This may however be unreliable information. This news was later confirmed by an original telegram and a second telegram again of December 1944. This telegram was a Christmas wish from van der Giessen to his parents.

As can be seen from this document, information changed regularly, and what was definite 'yesterday' was no more than just a 'maybe' today. The obvious question in relation to van der Giessen and van Rietschoten is if they did manage to return to Britain, why did they not subsequently make contact with the SOE and/or their parents after the Netherlands had been liberated? The fact that they did not make any contact with either adds weight to the theory that after they escaped from Haaren on the night of 22/23 November 1943, they were subsequently captured and then later shot dead on 10 June 1944.

The Dutch website www.englandspiel.eu states that three SOE agents, van der Giessen, Jan Jacob van Rietschoten and Antonious Johannes Wegner all escaped from Haaren on the night of 22/23 November 1943, a year earlier than shown in the SOE file. The website further states that van der Giessen and van Rietschoten were later captured and shot on 10 June 1944, near the town of Haerendael, whilst walking in the direction of Den Bosch, and that their bodies were later collected and cremated.

21 October 1942

Three men were parachuted into the Netherlands on 21 October 1942: Meindert Koolstra, Peter Kamphorst and Michiel Pals.

Meindert Koolstra was born on 4 June 1917 at Rinsumageest and was conscripted into the Dutch Army in 1936 before transferring to the mounted police in 1938. Having been transferred back to the Dutch Army in 1940, he subsequently undertook parachute training. He began his escape from the Netherlands to Britain on 15 May 1940 via Belgium and France, arriving on the south coast of England on 11 June.

After having been debriefed by British military intelligence, he was handed over to the Dutch authorities and as a serving soldier, was put to work by helping to safeguard Queen Wilhelmina of the Netherlands, who was living in exile in Britain.

On 18 June 1942, Koolstra became a member of the SOE. During his training he used the alias of Meindert Kolff, the name he used to sign his SOE 'declaration' in relation to his commitments under the Official Secrets Act. It was commonplace when using an alias for an agent to keep their Christian name, thus enabling them to react naturally if called by their name; a simple aspect of life as an SOE agent, which on active service could be the difference between life and death.

The SOE file on Koolstra makes for an interesting read. The following comments were made about him by members of the training staff on his initial course and describe the man in direct terms:

2 July 1942 – Corporals Boks and Mendes
A rather rougher type than the others, perhaps not altogether on the same education level.

9 July 1942 – Corporals Boks and Mendes
Progress is most satisfactory. Keenness and zeal as strong as ever. Very great team spirit.

11 July 1942 – Unnamed Instructor
Very capable and confident. A good man. Can be relied upon to do his job without any fuss.

16 July 1942 – Corporal Mendes
A good open-hearted fellow who will get on best with people of his own type (I mean of the same mental and cultural level; with others he has a tendency to feel awkward). Looks forward with appreciation to the work to come, especially its rougher aspects.

3 August 1942 – (1). Unnamed Instructor (2). Unnamed Commandant
(1). He has worked well on the course, and has reached good standards in all subjects, but there has been no enthusiasm at all, and he seemed bored.
(2). A solid reliable man. Could be trusted to carry through a job of work but does not seem to have imagination.

14 September 1942 – Unnamed Instructor

Not very intelligent but understands an idea clearly once he has got it into his head. A solid, reliable fellow, with little imagination or initiative, but who would carry out faithfully any job he was given. An attractive person upon whom one would rely on absolutely. Not very good at expressing his ideas, but nevertheless would perform his instructional duties thoroughly, and would also be capable of drawing up a plan of attack on a specific point, though not able to appreciate or plan action on a large scale.

16 October 1942 – Unnamed Instructor

Very sound and reliable. Not outstanding in any direction, but a most useful worker. Possibly a fair instructor.

It is interesting to note the varying comments made about Koolstra by his instructors, especially with comments such as, 'little imagination or initiative', 'not very good at expressing his ideas', 'not outstanding in any direction', but despite these comments, it was still deemed suitable to send him overseas. Indeed, the last of these comments was made only five days before he was parachuted into the Netherlands.

Koolstra was dropped near Ermelo in Gelderland on the night of 21 October 1942, and was immediately arrested by waiting Germans. Peter Kamphorst and Michiel Pals were also dropped on the same evening, but their landing location was some 9 miles away near the village of Voorhuizen. They were also met by waiting German soldiers as they landed and were immediately arrested.

Peter Kamphorst was born on 24 November 1894 at Ermelo, the exact same location where Koolstra would be dropped in October 1942. He served in the Dutch Army between 1914 and 1919 as a member of the Amersfoort Cavalry, before joining the mounted police after leaving the army in 1919, a role he still held when the country was overrun and occupied by rapidly advancing German forces in May 1940. At this time all Dutch military police units were instructed to escape and make their way to Britain where they were to assist the Dutch government operating out of London.

Having made his way to Britain, Kamphorst became a member of the SOE and began his training as an agent on 18 June 1942. During this time, he used the surname of Kerkhof, and as an agent in the field he also used the aliases Pieter van Wells, Pieter Kampenhorst, and Pieter van Putten. His code name was 'Eddie'.

What follows are comments made about Kamphorst contained in his SOE file:

2 July 1942 – Corporals Boks and Mendes
Has an amazing vitality for a man of his age. His physical qualifications outweigh however his mental capacity. Being of a certain age, he is of a calm and composed character. He is also very security conscious minded. Spends his free evenings having a few quiet drinks without over doing it.

9 July 1942 – Corporals Boks and Mendes
Progress most satisfactory. Keenness and zeal as strong as ever.

16 July 1942 – Corporal Mendes
Works hard, but owing to his age, it is far more difficult for him to pick up new efforts and ideas than it is for the others. All the same, he just carries on without feeling discouraged. Talks very little.

3 August 1942 – (1). Unnamed Instructor and (2). Commandant
(1). Despite some difficulties because he is the only student not able to follow English easily, he has kept up with the work remarkably well, and in practical work is as good as any of the others.

(2). An astounding man for his age. Despite his lack of formal education, he has mastered this new training. He is intelligent and thoughtful. A strong character, respected by the others.

14 September 1942 – Unnamed Instructor
Not outstandingly intelligent but has a good deal of common sense. His outstanding characteristic is his simplicity which means that though extremely reliable and thorough, he is incapable of planning anything but a simple operation and if under suspicion might find it difficult to mislead the police.

He would certainly be capable of putting across any technical instruction once he understood it and can be depended upon to let no one down."

16 October 1942 – Unnamed Instructor

A good solid and reliable type. An excellent worker, capable of sticking at any task and doing any work that he is given and that has been explained to him. Showed less suppleness and imagination than the rest of the party but worked in excellent co-operation with Doumam. This determination, thoroughness and common sense are qualities very useful in any party.

The comments contained within these reports are many and varied, and sometimes differ depending on who wrote them. One stated he was 'intelligent' whilst just over a month later he is described as being 'not outstandingly intelligent'.

Just five days after this final 'report' was placed on his personal file, he, too, was dropped into the Netherlands by parachute, and his war was over within minutes of landing. He was the oldest of the agents captured during Operation North Pole, being 49 years of age at the time of his death.

Michiel Pals was born on 4 May 1912 in the village of Hooge Zwaluwe. He enlisted in the Dutch Army in 1932 when he was just 20 years of age, and two years later transferred to the mounted police, before re-joining the Dutch Army in 1939, just before the outbreak of the Second World War. His unit made their way to Brest on the west coast of France, where he left by sea on 17 June 1940 and arrived in Plymouth the following day.

Whilst in England, and before becoming a member of the SOE, Pals was stationed at Porthcawl, Cobgleton, Stafford and Wrottersley Park in Wolverhampton. In November 1941, he underwent a two-month course as a tank wireless operator. He joined the SOE on 18 June 1942 and was designated as a wireless operator. The name he used during his training was Michel Post, and once active, he used the aliases of Marinus van de Plas and Michiel Post.

During his weeks of training, the following comments and observations were made about him by some of the instructors:

2 July 1942 – Corporals Boks and Mendes
Shows all the characteristics of the type of a regular soldier. Perhaps not one of the most intelligent of the party, but definitely a hard worker.

9 July 1942 – Corporals Boks and Mendes
Progress most satisfactory. Keenness and zeal as strong as ever. Shows very great team spirit.

11 July 1942 – (1). Unnamed Instructors (2). Commandant
(1). A very good student indeed. Learns quickly, has an acute and critical mind. Good standard in all subjects.
(2). A very good man. A good instructor, and with more training might make a good staff officer.

16 July 1942 – Corporals Boks and Mendes
In an all-round way, one of the best of the party. Gets on exceptionally well with the others. Is always in good spirits without being boisterous. Has a very steady and reflective character. Knowing him, one soon sees it is impossible to 'put something over on him'. He will always try and get to the bottom of any suggestion or problem with which he is confronted.

14 September 1942 – Unnamed Commandant's report
A very intelligent and level-headed man, in spite of the fact that he has had no great education. Extremely keen and energetic. Moreover, he gives great attention to detail. A most attractive personality, who inspires confidence and who has a good sense of humour. He would be very competent both at giving the instruction and in devising a plan of attack.

16 October 1942 – Unnamed Commandant
Intelligent, a good talker, a sound instructor and an excellent worker. Has a wide general knowledge, can appreciate a situation and plan carefully.

Again, it is interesting to note how individual impressions can differ so greatly. On 2 July Pals is described as 'not the most intelligent of the party', yet by 14 September he is described as being 'very intelligent', although, to be fair, they were opinions of different individuals.

After being captured, all three men were initially taken to the prison camp at Haaren that same day, where they remained for a period of time before being transferred to the prison camp in Rawicz. On 27 November 1943 they were transferred to Mauthausen, where they were murdered on 7 September 1944. The information about all three having been prisoners at Rawicz was confirmed when the SOE had contact from one of their French agents who had escaped from German captivity, and who reported seeing them at the prison camp at in July 1944.

Koolstra's parents were informed of their son's death by members of the Dutch Red Cross on 28 June 1945. He was posthumously awarded the Bronze Cross by the government of the Netherlands on 2 May 1953.

24 October 1942

Two agents were parachuted into the Netherlands on the evening of 24 October 1942, near the city of Steenwijk, in the Dutch province of Overijssel. They were Horst Reinder Steeksma, who also used the aliases Hendrik Reinder Versteeg, Horst Sevenster (used during his SOE training), and Horst Reinder. The other man who was dropped that evening was Humphrey Max Macaré. Both men were captured immediately after they landed.

Initially, both men were taken to a prison camp, located at the nearby town of Haaren, where they were held and interrogated. They remained there for a month before being moved to Mauthausen on 27 November 1943, where they were eventually executed on 7 September 1944.

Information received from a French SOE agent who escaped from the prison camp at Rawicz in July 1942, established that the two men were at the same camp at that time.

Steeksma was actually German by birth, having been born in Berlin on 14 October 1919, and somewhat ironically his parents and sister moved back to Berlin sometime around October 1939, where his father, Karel Klaus Steeksma, worked as an electrical engineer for AEG, which during the war worked closely with the Nazi Party and benefited from the use of forced labour and concentration camp prisoners.

For some inexplicable reason, the family's strong German connections were not seen as a potential security risk either by the SOE hierarchy or their counterparts as MI6. Afterall, Steeksma was a man who not only had his parents and sister living in the nation's capital, but his father worked for an organisation that had very strong links with the Nazi Party.

After having left the Netherlands on 17 May 1940 as part of the Dutch Army's 2nd Infantry Regiment, Steeksma made his way across Belgium and into France, before crossing the English Channel on 31 May 1940. He initially worked in an administrative capacity for H Company, Netherlands Brigade, before becoming a member of the SOE on 17 June 1942.

The following are the contents of reports that were written about Steeksma by his instructors during his training to become an agent for the SOE:

2 July 1942 – Corporals Boks and Mendes
Steeksma acts successfully as leader and representative of the group of NCOs. This is quite understandable owing to his rank and proficiency in PT and sports. His authority is accepted by the others. Doesn't know much of military training owing to the fact that previously in his own army, he has been holding a confidential clerical position. Learns very easily. On his evenings out, his main preoccupation is to seek the company of the opposite sex.

9 July 1942 – Corporals Boks and Mendes
This party is progressing most satisfactorily. Keenness and zeal are as strong as ever. Shows a very great team spirit. Steeksma and some of the others seem to have gathered quite a lot of information concerning our organisation and about the adventures experienced by people during their work for us. These rumours do not seem to have shaken their morals and determination.

The fact that the group had gone out of their way to garnish information about the organisation could well have been viewed in a negative sense, especially as Steeksma, who was seen by the others on his course as their de-facto leader, was born in Germany and whose family were living in Germany at the time and had connections with the Nazis. However, having discovered this information, the SOE did not appear at all concerned.

17 July 1942 – Corporal Mendes
Shows great team spirit with rest of party. Previously it was stated that he was looked upon by the other NCOs as their leader. I have nethertheless observed that when officially appointed to exert his authority, he only does so very reluctantly and fails to make a great impression. In other words, his leadership which was mentioned on the previous occasion, only applies to his excellence for physical tests and far less from the point of view of a dominating character.

It is interesting to note how much of what the students did on the course, whether it was whilst under instruction, or in their own time, was noticed by the training staff, which allowed them to form an in-depth opinion of each of the students.

5 August 1942 – Corporal Mendes
Lacks security mindedness. Far too impulsive in thought and action. Only realises his mistakes after being told. To give an example: At 'dromo', calls over to us a fellow countryman, ex-friend from his camp to exchange greetings with him. The result was that real names were used during the ensuing conversation in the presence of Kamphorst. In view of the possibility that the latter may be withdrawn from the course, it was rather imperative that he should not have got to know a single identity of the others. Steeksma has sought the company of women at dances.

The above incident resulted in Corporal Mendes sending a report to the course Commandant on 14 August:

Steeksma required extremely careful handling with regard to future security training as his background, even though it was confidential, does not seem to have given him much practical experience of security in the field. FSP's final report in which it is stated, 'he only realises his mistakes after being told' is an example of how dangerous this man could be if he is not carefully trained.

Would you therefore consider his case carefully before sending him on for further training, and if you do send him on, he should be warned most specifically that should he fail to satisfy our requirements with regard to security and the objects for which he is being trained, his future activities would have to form the subject of very serious consideration.

The comments of Corporal Mendes are close to asking that Steeksma be removed from the course, without actually asking for it to be done, but despite his observations and recommendations, this did not take place. The following two reports are by different course Commandants, who quite clearly have very different opinions of Steeksma. Indeed, the second of the two is very much opposed to the report by Corporal Mendes of 14 August.

14 September 1942 – SOE training establishment STS 31 – Commandant's report

Extremely intelligent and quick-witted. Very keen and hard working. He has, however, one constantly recurring fault, that of jumping to conclusions and into hasty action without sufficient thought. It is a question of whether this combination of courage and hastiness would not make him more suitable for a type of Commando activity, rather than for slow patient work of a clandestine nature. He has a pleasant personality; but most people would not consider him to be a very consistent or reliable superior.

That could not especially be classed as a glowing report and is leaning very heavily towards finding Steeksma unsuitable for the work he was being trained for. With that in mind, how the conclusions could have been arrived at in the next report, is unclear.

16 October 1942 – SOE training establishment STS 17 – Commandant's report
Keen, intelligent, and thorough. He showed throughout the course a high degree of initiative and resource, coupled with common sense. Could be relied on to do any work thoroughly. Appeared capable of both instructing and planning.

It would appear that there was sufficient doubt concerning Steeksma's overall abilities to suggest that he was not really a suitable candidate to work as an agent who would be required to work slowly and methodically behind enemy lines. He was undoubtedly a brave and competent young man, but as was said in the first of the two reports, his individual skills could have been put to better use as a Commando. Despite this, the decision was still taken by senior members of the SOE to send him to work as an agent in the Netherlands. Maybe there was a lack of agents, and it was simply a case of 'needs must' in wartime.

Humphrey Max Macaré was born on 12 October 1921 in Bandoeng, in what was the Dutch East Indies, where his father worked on the railways. After completing his education, he decided he wanted to remain in the Far East and become a teacher, but that career path was cut short when, despite being only 5 feet 2 inches tall, he was conscripted into the Dutch Navy in July 1941. In the Navy he was trained as a telegrapher, which no doubt helped him to eventually become a wireless operator in the SOE.

After Japanese forces invaded and occupied Java on 1 March 1942, all Dutch military forces were evacuated from the region two days later. Initially, Macaré found himself in Colombo, Sri Lanka, but on 17 March, he managed to board the Dutch troopship MS *Nieuw-Amsterdam* and make his way to England, where he finally arrived on 3 May. He was first sent to the main Dutch military training facility at Wrottesley Park, but on 6 June 1942, just over a month later, he became a member of the SOE. During his training he used the surname of Mebins. Another alias he used was Barend Merens.

The following reports were made about him by members of the SOE training staff:

2 July 1942 – Corporals Boks and Mendes
Very happy in his new way of life. He seems to consider it a privilege to have been accepted in this service and appears very grateful. He is doing his utmost to keep pace with the others as far as military training is concerned even though he gets less of it and had to start from scratch.

9 July 1942 – Corporals Boks and Mendes
Very subdued sort of chap and very shy. Doesn't speak to anybody outside our party if not compelled to. Will probably get good results on the training, but his keenness for going on the real job seems, for the moment, to depend on the place where he will eventually be sent. His interests are entirely centred round the colonies.

16 July 1942 – Corporal Boks
Shyness is this man's chief characteristic. He never mixes with anybody he doesn't know. He comes out with us and goes in for the same things as we do, but in a contemplative way, as if it didn't really affect him although he is interested in it from an objective point of view. Whether he is security minded or not is hard to tell, you cannot penetrate his feelings or his ideas, but one thing is certain, he doesn't run many risks in the security line and he is not the sort to do anything foolish or act without thinking.

For the kind of work Macaré was training for, his outward persona appears to have been ideal, no doubt greatly assisted by his inherent shyness which naturally prevented him from opening up and divulging too much information about himself.

After being captured, Macaré and Steeksma were taken to the old seminary at Haaren, where before the war young Dutch men had gone in preparation for becoming priests. Macaré remained at Haaren until 27 November 1943, when he was moved to a prison in Assen, just 30 miles from the German border. In April 1944 he was moved again, this time to the camp at Rawicz. It is believed he was executed there on 30 April 1944 along with six other Dutch SOE agents: Jacob Bakker, Adriaan Mooy, Felix Dono Ortt, Hermanus Parlevliet and Charles Christiaan Pouwels.

24 October 1942

The two SOE agents Jan Hofstede and Charles Christiaan Pouwels were dropped near the village of Holten, which is located in the Salland region of the Netherlands and were arrested by German forces immediately upon landing.

Charles Christiaan Pouwels was born in the city of Padang Panjan, Indonesia, on 25 September 1923. He joined the SOE on 18 June 1942 and during his basic training went by the name of Christian Praag. Prior to the outbreak of the war, he had worked as an office clerk; becoming an agent with the SOE was as far removed from his previous line of work as it was possible to get.

Pouwels' SOE file contained varied information about him, including the following comments made by his trainers and commanding officer:

2 July 1942 – Corporals Boks and Mendes

Very happy in his new way of life. Seems to consider it a privilege to have been accepted into this service and appears very grateful. He is doing his utmost to keep pace with the others as far as military training is concerned even though he got less of it and had to start from scratch. His main sympathies to all appearances, go out far more to the Colonies than to the Motherland.

9 July 1942 – Corporals Boks and Mendes

Very quiet sort of chap. Does not go out at every opportunity. His father got some sort of university degree in Germany, and I understand it was German that was spoken quite often at his home. While his friends here are keen on improving their English, he doesn't bother because he admits openly that he doesn't like English people in general without being able to state any reasons, and that it is very improbable that he will have anything to do with them after this war.

Reading this report some eighty years after it was written immediately raises alarm bells as to whether it was right that Pouwels should have been accepted into such a secretive organisation as the SOE. Here was a man who spoke fluent German, had no desire to learn, or improve, his English, and freely admitted that he did not like English people in general, and that it was more than probable he would have nothing to do with them after the war.

16 July 1942 – Corporal Boks

Moderate drinker and smoker. Seems to like a calm and peaceful life. He is not keen on going out and does so only when he has a special reason. He likes to keep himself to himself.

During their training, potential agents were required to live at people's homes rather than in barracks style accommodation. On a specific date, and unbeknown to the students, the house in question was visited by members of the SOE training staff to carry out unannounced security checks on the property. The following is the report submitted to Major Lee:

Undated – Sergeants Stebbing and Allen and Company Sergeant Major Cripps

An unexpected raid was made upon the house in which the above named student (Pouwels, one of four students), was residing. These students had been doing no 'security' work whilst staying this time in Newcastle and did not realise that anyone might descend on their house. The two organisers were let into the house by the house holder and went upstairs without having their presence made known to the one student (Praag) who was at the time in the house.

The work room was entered, and it was found that the wireless set had been left in complete array by the last user and no attempt had been made to hide its presence nor had the door of the room been locked. Anyone could have entered the room and would have found the reason for the presence of the students in the house. A search was then made of the students' rooms and belongings. Their work papers, messages, etc, were lying about and no attempt had been made to tidy up or to hide their existence. Papers had been left in chests of drawers and in unlocked attaché cases. In the case of Lieutenant Starup, he had left in his room a locked brief-case, but all his papers had been put away in an unlocked chest of drawers.

The main reason for Pouwels and his colleagues having been housed in such accommodation was to try to replicate the conditions they would find themselves in as active agents. The possibility of local Gestapo officers turning up announced at their location was a real one, and if similar items were so easily found, the outcome would have more than likely been fatal for those concerned.

29 September 1942 – Report on scheme at Newcastle. Home of Mrs Kinnersley, The Red House, Stocksfield, Newcastle
A previous report on this student was not altogether favourable. He showed considerable improvements on this scheme. His confidence has increased and he is much more a master of himself. Some exercises were particularly well done though he ruined a whole afternoon's work by failing to arrive at the RV at the correct time. For this he was severely reprimanded.

It would appear that Pouwels had learned from his experience at Mrs Ashforth's, as the report also noted that he, 'is security minded, discreet in his demeanour, and careful in the disposal of his set and papers.'

After his arrest following his landing in the Netherlands, Pouwels was taken to the prison camp at Haaren where he remained until he was transferred to Rawicz on 27 November 1943. He was executed there on 30 April 1944, along with fellow Dutch agents, Adriaan Mooy, Jacob Bakker, Humphrey Max Macaré, Felix Dono Ortt, Frederik Willem Rouwerd and Hermanus Parlevliet.

Jan Hofstede was born on 17 December 1918 at Bilthoven. He was one of ten children, with four sisters and five brothers. An intelligent young man, he was both sporty and academic, as well as able to speak Dutch, English and German. He was just 20 years of age when he was conscripted into the Dutch Army in January 1938, but a year later he transferred to the Dutch Navy and became a sailor in the coastal vessel unit. This was also short lived as in September 1939 he was mobilised before being discharged in June 1940 and conscripted into the Reconstruction Service in August 1940, where he remained for the following four months. He arrived in England in mid-October 1941 and joined the SOE on 14 June 1942. The bulk of his course was undertaken at the STS 6 training location.

His SOE file includes the following reports written by members of the SOE's training staff:

2 July 1942 – Corporals Boks and Mendes
Though very keen and intelligent the impression one gets after knowing him a while is that he has a marked tendency to attract attention to his own person. Has mixed well with the others, managing to make friends with them without giving away information concerning himself. Not as disciplined from a military point of view.

9 July 1942 – Corporals Boks and Mendes
Progress most satisfactory. Keenness and zeal as strong as ever. Very great team spirit.

16 July 1942 – Corporal Mendes
Keen worker. Example: He was the only one who was upset when told that this course would be shorter than first anticipated. His argument was 'one cannot get enough training for this kind of work'. The others hailed the same news with satisfaction, not because they object to the training, but because we are in such a solitary spot.

5 August 1942 – Corporal Mendes
Hofstede has sought the company of women at dances.

There was no explanation as to the reason for this latter observation. Was it because it was seen as a weakness, or a worry that if he conducted himself in the same manner whilst on active service behind enemy lines, it could potentially place him in a vulnerable position resulting in his capture and interrogation?

14 September 1942 – Unnamed Instructor

Average intelligence; very keen and reliable. An attractive personality and one who would inspire confidence. He should be able to carry out his instructional job without difficulty and also to plan operations on a small scale. During the scheme he showed a tendency to do his job adequately but mechanically and without any real thought.

The last sentence in particular is actually quite astounding, as taking those comments at face value, it would appear that individuals such as Hofstede did not appear to grasp the seriousness of what their training was preparing them for. The concept that they were soon to be operating behind enemy lines, and that if they were not totally focused on what they had to do at all times, they would more than likely be captured by the Germans, interrogated, tortured and executed.

The other worrying aspect of the training prospective SOE agents had to undertake was the different subjective opinions made by members of the different training teams. By way of example, Hofstede is referred to as having different levels of intelligence. In July 1942, whilst at STS 6, he is said to be of average intelligence, but the following month, in August, at STS 24, he is described as being intelligent. Finally, in September, he is described as 'average' while at STS 34.

It cannot be possible to obtain a clear picture of a student's true overall abilities, and suitability to work as an agent in the field, when different instructors view their levels of intelligence differently. There is every possibility that some students who were parachuted into the Netherlands were not actually suitable, and therefore should have never been sent.

28 October 1942

On this date, Jacob Bakker and Johannes Cornelis Dane were dropped into the Netherlands at Holten, and immediately captured and arrested.

Jacob Bakker was born on 1 May 1917 at Batavia, where he lived and attended school until he was 15, after which time his parents moved to Velsen. After completing his full-time secondary education, he attended the Seaman's School in Amsterdam, an establishment for young men who wanted to serve in the Dutch Merchant Navy and spent the next two years learning his chosen profession.

Desperate to escape his occupied country and make his way to England, Bakker, along with a number of his friends, left the Netherlands on board the hijacked Dutch trawler *Katwijk LL*, on 7 April 1942, and arrived the following day at Great Yarmouth. On his arrival, he was interrogated by members of British military intelligence, and his story of escape because of his desire to continue the fight against Germany was believed.

He became a member of the SOE on 18 May 1942, and during his period of training he used the alias of Jacob Willems.

It would be fair to say that reports made about him by his instructors during his training were far from complimentary. One such report by Sergeant Holland, dated 15 September 1942, just a month before he was dropped into the Netherlands, included the following comments:

His manner is impetuous and hasty, and he is easily ruffled. He is however keen, and willing to learn. He has no imagination and very little common sense. He was unable to adapt himself to the circumstances under which he was working. He tried hard enough and readily admitted his faults but seemed unable to apply sufficient intelligence to rectify his faults.

Yet again, a report on an individual which brings into question their suitability to become an effective and competent agent in the field. This was not a game. This literarily was a case of life and death.

The exact date and location of Bakker's death remain a mystery. It is known that he arrived at the prison camp at Haaren on 30 October 1942, where he remained until November 1943 when he was then transferred to a prison camp at Assen, before ending up at Rawicz in April 1944. Just a month later, nearly all of the agents held at Rawicz were transferred to Mauthausen. One of those who was not part of the group, however, was Bakker.

In 1953, Bakker was posthumously awarded the Bronze Cross for his wartime sacrifice by the Dutch authorities.

Bakker's colleague, Johannes Cornelis Dane was born on 27 April 1912 in Axel. He enlisted in the Dutch Army in November 1937 and was initially stationed in Middelburg, where he worked in an administrative capacity. In 1938 he became an instructor in the artillery, at the training establishment in Bergen Op Zoom, but the following year became a member of the Dutch mounted police in Apeldoorn.

He enlisted in the SOE on 18 June 1942, and during his period of training went by the alias of Johannes Cornelis Douma. Whilst still undergoing his training to be an agent, he married Gwyneth Jane Margeriet, meaning that between getting married and being deployed on active service, Dane and his bride had spent less than two months together. Despite this relatively short period of time, a daughter, who Dane never saw, was born the following year. It is likely he never even knew his wife was pregnant.

The first of the reports compiled on Dane was completed less than a month after he joined the SOE:

2 July 1942 – Corporals Boks and Mendes
On the whole a satisfactory student; rather on the chatty side owing to certain childish traits in his character, especially noticeable to his letters to his English fiancée. One of the reasons for his desire to get into our Service is that he had certain misunderstandings with his own officers. His father who was with him in the same Army, maybe partly to blame for this as one of his ambitions was to see his son get a Commission.

The course instructors, along with the Commandant of the training course, all saw Dane as an intelligent and competent individual, who was well thought of by all who knew him. Indeed, the Commandant wrote the following of him on 3 August 1942: 'Probably the best NCO student we have on the course. A very determined and forceful man. When first meeting him, you would be forgiven for thinking that he was all muscle and no brain, but I think he has more brains than any of the other students on the course.'

He was thought of so highly by his instructors, who had never had such an all-round accomplished student on their course, that they felt he was suitable to be a future instructor.

Physically, Dane was nearly 6 feet 2 inches tall and weighed just under 14 stone. He was a powerfully built and a fascinating individual, who some might even describe as being intimidating.

After his initial capture, Dane was interrogated at the local police station before being imprisoned at the old seminary at Haaren on 30 October 1942. It is known that between being held at Haaren and Mauthausen, he also spent time at Rawicz prison camp. He died at Mauthausen on 7 September 1944; one of those who was 'shot whilst trying to escape'.

28 November 1942

Arie Johannes de Kruijff and George Lodewijk Ruseler were dropped in the skies over the village of Ugchelen on the evening of 28 November 1942, and were both immediately arrested by the Germans. After being interrogated at the local police station, they were taken to the prison camp at Haaren on 30 November. Both men met their death on 7 September 1944 at Mauthausen.

Arie Johannes de Kruijff was born on 16 November 1912 in Amsterdam. He was a married man, and at the time of his enlistment in the SOE on 15 July 1942, his wife and recently born son were living at an address in Johannesburg, South Africa.

The file held by the SOE on de Kruijff contained a number of reports, most of which were in relation as to how he was doing on his training course. One of these reports was written by Sergeant van Blankenstein and dated 4 September 1942. At the time, de Kruijff's training had taken him to Dunham House in Altrincham, Cheshire where trainee SOE agents went for parachute training. Whilst in training he used the alias of Arie Johaanes de Klijn, and having passed the course he also used the surname of Kuyper, with his code name being 'Elst'.

4 September 1942 – Sergeant Van Blankenstein
This student is more excitable; he is highly strung, nervous, very stubborn, but has a real sound character. He is straight forward and reliable. Does not drink. He is a man of fixed ideas; when he has made up his mind about something, nothing can make him change it. He is security minded. He goes out seldom and has no interest in women.

George Lodewijk Ruseler was born on 27 February 1922 at Surabaya, Indonesia. Prior to the war, he had been a wireless operator in the Dutch Navy, and joined the SOE on 18 June 1942, using the alias of George Rutgers during basic training.

Whilst at STS 6 in Berkshire, the following was written about Ruseler by two members of the training staff. Interestingly, the first of Ruseler's reports is exactly the same as one of Macaré's, and even includes the exact same wording. This is highlighted simply to clarify that these are factual entries in the records and not a result of an error or oversight on the part of the author.

2 July 1942 – Corporals Boks and Mendes
Very happy in his new way of life. He seems to consider it a privilege to have been accepted in this Service and appears very grateful. He is doing his utmost to keep pace with the others as far as military training is concerned even though he gets less of it and had to start from scratch.

The following report relates to his time spent at STS 52 at Thame Park in Oxfordshire, where perspective SOE agents were trained to be wireless operators:

16 July 1942 – Corporal Boks
Carefree cheerful young man. He takes everything with a smile and always looks at the best side of things. He has assimilated all of the sound security advice given to him and tries hard to remember it; for the rest, he hopes for the best. Anyway, he is endowed with a fair amount of common sense that should keep him out of mischief.

As previously discussed, it was usual for agents to spend time living and working out of a civilian home to give them some idea of what it would be like once they were working behind enemy lines in occupied Holland. Compare the difference in what is written about Ruseler above to some of those that followed. The first report, which is dated 29 September 1942, came after he had stayed at the home of Mrs Kinnerley, in Stocksfield:

> This student is very immature. He had to be coached in every exercise he did and shown exactly how to attempt them. He was bewildered by a large city, and this made him timid and shy in all his actions. He needs abundant practice in every type of exercise.
>
> Security wise he is discreet both in his conversation and in his behaviour. He fully realises the importance of security and is keen to learn all he can.

The second report is dated 13 October 1942, less than six weeks before he was dropped into Holland to carry out his mission and was in relation to his stay at the home of Mrs Ashforth, in Jesmond.

> Due to the short period the student and myself worked together on the above scheme, I do not feel justified in making any definitive comments on the student, beyond saying I had the impression that he did not seem to take the work seriously enough, despite my stressed observations on all angles of the scheme. Although, as will be seen, he did fairly well, there was an air of disinterested resignation about him.

A later report also commented on the fact that 'there was a marked improvement in his work, but it is thought most unlikely that he will ever attain the standard of efficiency and competency required.'

The obvious question here, is how did a young man whose instructors felt was so below the standard required for an agent, suddenly improve so dramatically that he was deemed suitable to be sent on an important mission behind enemy lines?

Nevertheless, Ruseler was posthumously awarded the Bronze Cross for his war time service on 6 June 1953.

29 November 1942

Johan Bernard Ubbink and Herman Johannes Overes left on their mission on the evening of 29 November 1942 and were dropped into the Netherlands in the early hours of 30 November at Leersum and immediately arrested by waiting German forces. Ubbink would eventually escape from captivity on 29 August 1943 and make his way back to England. Overes, however, was not so fortunate.

Johan Bernard Ubbink was born on 22 May 1921 in the city of Doesburg, and in the early stages of the war had been a member of the Dutch Merchant Navy between October 1940 and September 1941. In November 1941 he joined the Dutch Royal Navy, with whom he remained until May 1942. He was intelligent, especially in languages where he could speak Dutch, German, English and a little French. He was also quite a sporty individual who enjoyed sailing, swimming and hockey.

He began training as an SOE agent on 22 May 1942 and used the alias of Bernard Udema. Ubbink's SOE file is quite substantial and includes information about his escape from the Netherlands after his arrest, making his way back to England, and his subsequent incarceration in Brixton prison in London on his return.

His SOE file, which runs to twenty-three pages in length, begins with an undated two-paged typed statement signed by Ubbink. He begins by explaining how he and other captured agents were suspicious of an agent only referred to by the code name of 'Bingham', the inference being that he was a double agent working for the Germans. Having made mention of Bingham, he emphasises that he has no evidence against him, but that he personally suspects him of having committed an unexplained blight against the SOE and the organisation's Dutch agents.

Ubbink mentioned in his statement that when he was interrogated in The Hague by officers of the German SD, the only person that they did not ask for a description of was Bingham, which only raised his suspicions about the man even higher than they had been before. Another point that he made, and with the benefit of hindsight one that appears to have been obvious, was why the SOE hierarchy did not recall the agents they had dropped into Holland to spend leave in London, which would also ensure they were doing the work they were claiming to have done and had not been captured and fallen into the hands of the Germans.

Ubbink also raises the point about some of those who were selected as agents. Although Dutch by birth, many of them were far too young and inexperienced to be effective agents. Some had not lived in the Netherlands for many years, and those who had lived and been educated in the Dutch East Indies generally had a darker skin colour than would have been expected of a Dutch man living in Rotterdam or Amsterdam over a similar period of time. Ubbink told how he knew of one individual from the Dutch East Indies who was deemed suitable to be an agent for the SOE, but who could not tie a tie and did not know how to use a telephone. He also said that the German officers who worked in military intelligence found it hard to understand how 'such people were sent out to do such very important and dangerous work'.

Ubbink said that he had spoken with British intelligence officers whilst in Spain who were 'very indignant' about the fact that the 'people in England' were sending people to work behind enemy lines, who clearly had no understanding of 'the difficulties connected with operating in occupied territory'. The inference being that those responsible for the training of SOE agents in Britain had a major failing in that they might know the theory, but had not experienced at first hand the very work they were training others to do.

The following is from a report made by Ubbink on 19 December 1943 at the Netherlands Embassy in Madrid, Spain. It is of great value as it gives a first-hand account not only of the pre-flight preparation, but what happened in the immediate aftermath of landing on Dutch soil and the subsequent capture by the Germans: 'We obtained our papers in the afternoon of the 29th November together with instructions for Holland which consisted of seeking contact with the leader of the reception committee who would be present at the spot where we would land by parachutes.'

He went on to explain that before they left for the aerodrome, they ate a hearty meal at STS 61, which was at Gaynes' Hall, Cambridgeshire. It almost sounds like a description of the 'last supper'. They were joined by a Captain Bingham, which I believe is a reference to Seymour Bingham, the man in charge of the SOE's Dutch section, and the person of whom Ubbink was suspicious. After dinner, the two men spoke and Ubbink recalls how Bingham told him that he should not 'underestimate the Germans, especially the ones who worked in counterespionage as they are very well trained'. Ubbink could not help but think this was a very strange thing for somebody to say, especially one who held such a position as Bingham did at the time.

The following is Ubbink's personal account of his landing in Holland and what happened in the immediate moments afterwards:

At 4 o'clock we arrived over the spot where we would jump and after Overes jumped from the plane on the sign 'despatcher'. The landing place was near Amerongen in the province of Utrecht. After I had reached the ground I discarded my parachute-costume and reconnoitred the surroundings.

After some time, I heard somebody call my code-name 'Louis', which was a sign for me to make myself known according to instructions from England, which I did. So, I came into contact with this person, who helped me to take down the parachute, which had become entangled in a tree. This person made himself known as the leader of the reception committee and congratulated me with the safe landing. After that he asked me whether I was armed to which I replied in the affirmative. He proposed to hand the weapon to him for the reason that I would certainly be arrested if I was stopped by the German police. I consented, after I had refused at first, He then enquired after Major Eland and after the situation in England regarding the food position etc.

We then walked to a spot outside the wood where I landed to find my colleague Overes with about another 5 members of the reception committee. When we arrived there the leader asked me for my real name to obtain a real identity card which could be classified under my real name. He would see to it that I obtained a current identity card which he would obtain illegally. This would be much safer for me according to the leader as the identity card given to me in England was not correct and notably bad.

It was about this time of the proceedings that Ubbink started to feel something was not quite right, putting him in an extremely difficult situation.

As I did not understand this logic and also had received orders not to enter into particulars with the leader, I declared my dissatisfaction with this proposal and refused to give my name; my colleague however gave his. At this moment I began to feel less at ease although I did not doubt the correctness of the intentions of the reception committee, as they knew our correct code-names and were able to name officers and acquaintances of the organisation.

The leader of the reception committee appears to have been quite calm and intent on engaging Ubbink in conversation, some of which seemed out of place and irrelevant to the situation they were in. It was more than likely a ploy to relax Ubbink into revealing facts about himself and the SOE: 'While we stood talking on a small path along the wood, other members of the reception committee were busy searching for the 6 containers and 2 radio sets which had been dropped from the plane together with us.'

The parachutes belonging to Ubbink and Overes, along with their torches, knifes and compasses were buried in a nearby pre-dug hole. Ubbink could not help but notice the sudden lack of any more questions, coupled with an almost eerie silence:

Then we were suddenly seized from behind by two persons who immediately handcuffed us, after which the cloven feet appeared and the pseudo reception committee showed itself up and appeared to be in the service of the German 'Sicherheitsdienst'.

They told us that the people in England did not take counterintelligence into account, and that the entire organisation was in the hands of the 'Sicherheitsdienst' and that these provocated [sic] the people in England in an excellent way. I did not believe this but later on it turned out to be true. One of the men left us and later on returned with German Gestapo officers and soldiers, who had completely surrounded the woods. We were taken under guard of the reception committee and German officers, whereas the containers, etc, were loaded in a truck. All this took some time but at 7 o'clock in the morning of 1 December 1943, we drove to The Hague to an office of the Sicherheitsdienst installed in one of the former Government buildings.

At no time during this detailed account of what happened to him from the moment he landed on Dutch soil did Ubbink make any mention of his state of mind, the emotions he experienced, or any shock and surprise he felt at having been unexpectedly handcuffed and detained.

His account of arriving in The Hague continued:

There I was offered coffee and cigarettes which I accepted as I smoke a lot and the emotion of that morning made a cigarette a welcome object of diversion, especially as my brain had to work at a feverish pace. Then the chief of the reception committee came to me and the handcuffs were fixed to the arms of the chair. I gave him my name, date and place of birth.

During his subsequent interview, Ubbink was asked for the names and addresses of the people he was to make contact with if there was no reception committee waiting for him when he landed in Holland. This he refused to do, but unfortunately for the individuals concerned, Ubbink's partner, Overes, was not so resilient.

Ubbink's interrogation was carried out by Untersturmführer Laur of the SD. At first, he refused to answer any questions put to him, but Ubbink said that Laur told him it served no purpose to remain silent as they already knew everything. He provided Ubbink with a list of the names of the other agents who had been part of his course, although the names were not included in the report. Ubbink further claimed that Laur also provided him with a list of the locations and dates of where he had undergone his SOE training, along with 'who the intelligence and other officers were', but he did not, however, mention if Laur had told him the actual numbers of these locations.

Ubbink also remarked that Laur told him he had information about the locations of 'all of the eight training schools' and that they even had sketches of each down to 'the smallest detail'. The problem with this is that the SOE had a total of eighteen experimental stations, and a minimum of at least sixty training schools and other locations. The point here is that Ubbink did not know the number of SOE locations or where they were located, because other than the ones he attended during his training, he did not need to know. This means that Laur could have told him there were any number of training schools and he would have been none the wiser.

Ubbink claimed in his report that he did not initially give up his radio code, but eventually did so, 'perhaps from cowardice' and only after having been interrogated for nearly five days with very little in the way of sleep. During his interrogation he claims he was shown the detailed reports made by other captured agents but does not mention their names.

He arrived at the seminary of the Catholic church at Haaren on the evening of 5 December 1942 and was allocated cell number 52. Overes was placed next to him in cell number 53. Ubbink said that there were two agents in cell number 51, who said their names were Louwers and Vulkaam and that they had been held there for about a year. At first, he was unsure if they were who they said they were, or if they were Dutch traitors pretending to be captured agents in an effort to get them to reveal bits of information they had not mentioned when interrogated.

Ubbink spoke of how he and Overes were treated during their stay, that they were heavily guarded all the time, which made attempting to escape extremely difficult. By looking out of his cell window down into what had become the exercise yard, he came to recognise a number of others who were also being held in the camp.

Having been in the camp for about ten weeks, Overes was moved into Ubbink's cell, but on 26 May 1943 they were both placed in cell number 45 along with a third captured SOE agent, Pieter Arendse, which led him to discover that Pieter Dourlein, Pieter Bleeker and Klaas van de Bor, were in cell number 46. Being neighbours resulted in Ubbink and Dourlein becoming close friends, to such a degree that they decided to attempt an escape.

Their first attempt took place on 28 August and was a failure, but they tried again the next day and were successful. The corridor on which their cells were situated was guarded by three men Monday to Friday, but during the course of the weekend, this was reduced to only one. Each evening at 8 o'clock, all the prisoners had to take off their clothes and leave them in the corridor outside their cells. The time the two men had chosen to make their escape was just after half past five, when they were given their evening meal, although on most occasions this was nothing more substantial than a piece of bread. Each of the cells was opened one at a time, the bread was handed over, and the cell door was shut again before the next one was opened. To be able to hand the bread out in one go, the guards had it on a wooden trolley with wheels. One guard would push the trolley whilst the other would unlock each of the cells. The good thing about this was that the combination of guards, the trolley and the opening and closing of cell doors meant an accompanying noise came with the process.

Above each of the cell doors was a window and Dourlein and Ubbink decided this was the way they would get out of the cell, using the noise that went with feeding time to mask their escape. The corridor outside the cells was a square with two corners, giving it a 'U' shape. Although the window to their cell was closed, in the days leading up to the escape the men had forced it loose with an iron rod they had removed from their bed. To make the cells even more secure there were bars in front of the glass, but because of the weight both men had lost it was possible to wriggle through the bars. The cell next to theirs was unoccupied and also left unlocked. Whilst the guards were out of sight delivering the bread to the other cells, the two men removed the window in their cell, slipped through the bars and hid in the neighbouring cell. When the guards left, Dourlein and Ubbink walked along the corridor until they came to a cloakroom which contained three toilets for the guards. Each of the toilets had a window with bars on the outside. They selected the furthest toilet from the entrance to the cloakroom, guessing that this would be the one that was least used, and hid in there until it was gone midnight. To assist with their escape, both men had spent time making a rope from the cover of their mattresses. Tied together, the ropes measured nearly 25 metres in length. After removing the glass and carefully squeezing through the gaps between the bars, both men lowered themselves to the ground outside the toilet block, a drop of about 10 metres. They then loosened the rope and bundled it up before dropping it in a nearby drain. But their escape was far from over.

Next, they carefully made their way over three barbed wire obstacles, trying to be as quiet as possible so as not to draw the attention of the guards. Their final hurdle before they were free was to swim across a small canal which ran along one side of the camp. Once free they then made their way to Tilburg, a distance of about 8 miles. Fortunately, one of their fellow prisoners at Haaren, Jan Christiaan Kist, had provided them with a name and address of a friend of his in Tilburg, a Mr Mutsaerts, who owned the town's chemist shop. By the time the two men arrived in the town the shop was shut. Rather than hang around and possibly draw attention to themselves, they made their way to the church where they spoke with the priest. They were now in dangerous territory as they had absolutely no idea of the allegiances of anybody who they chose to speak to. The priest took them to a man called Mr van Bilsen, who had been a police inspector in nearby Ginneken but had been discharged from his duties after having refused to collaborate with occupying German forces. Living in Tilburg, he worked for the Dutch underground press and was the editor of the illegal newspaper, *The Voice of the Free Netherlands*.

On 30 August, van Bilsen took the two men to a farm in the nearby village of Moergestel, where they remained for the following ten days. Whilst there they managed to get a message to London, with the help of local members of the Dutch resistance. The reply they received was not what they were hoping for, being told to remain where they were if they could not escape to a neutral country.

On the evening of 10 September 1943, they were taken back to Tilburg to the home of the Lauwerijssen family, with whom they stayed until 24 October. After that they stayed with another local family for a week, before staying at the home of Mr van Bilsen. All these individuals were extremely brave in what they did, because if their actions had come to the attention of the Germans, it would have had dire consequences. Whilst at van Bilsen's home, Ubbink managed to make contact with his brother, who worked for Dutch underground organisations. He came to visit him and revealed how their home had been raided by the Germans on the day he had escaped. Both his mother and two sisters had been arrested and taken to the police prison in Arnhem, whilst German soldiers had remained in the house waiting for him to return.

On 11 November Ubbink and Dourlein left the safety of van Bilsen's home and began their journey towards Switzerland. It would be fair to say that neither of them were happy with the response they received from London. From Tilburg they made their way to the Dutch-Belgian border and crossed at the village of Poppel. Once in Belgium they travelled on to Antwerp and from there made their way to Brussels before arriving in Mons. On the morning of 13 November, they crossed into France by train and arrived in Paris later that afternoon. After spending a few days in the French capital and then travelling by bus and train, they arrived at Maché, where on the night of 18/19 November they crossed the border into Switzerland and from there they made their way to Bern, where they were initially interrogated by British intelligence officers at the British Legation, before meeting with the Legation's Military Attaché, Major General van Tricht. Once the men's story was believed, arrangements were made for their return to England.

Their return to England was not a happy one because rather than being treated like heroes and congratulated on their heroic and brave escape from German-occupied Holland, on 27 May 1944 they were arrested and, without any form of trial, were detained in Brixton prison in London under a detention order issued by a Principal Secretary of State at the Home Office and dated 23 May 1944. During his detention, Ubbink wrote a letter to Colonel de Bruyne, an officer who served with the Royal Dutch Marines.

Sir,
For the last time I ask your attention in the matter in which Dourlein and I are concerned.

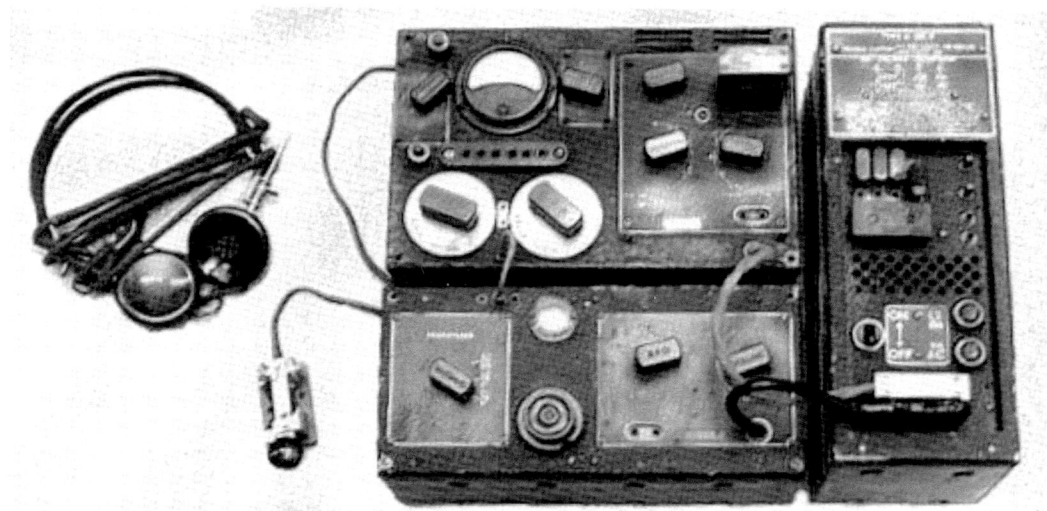

A Kofferset radio used by SOE agents in the Netherlands.

Left and below: Lysander aircraft used for dropping operatives during Operation North Pole.

Opposite and above: SOE agents during their training before deployment.

Below left: Parachute training.

Below right: Specially adapted handgun for members of the SOE.

Right: The infamous Stairs of Death at Mauthausen concentration camp.

Below: Memorial to the SOE agents murdered at Mauthausen.

Above: Plaque to SOE Operative Humphrey Max Macaré.

Below: Plaque at what was once the SOE's headquarters in the City of Westminster.

On 27 of May we are arrested and detained in Brixton Prison without any form of trial. I included the detention order which was given to us when we were arrested.

It is clear we are not trusted. I want to explain that if the people who did this to us got information out of Occupied Country, the information was given by the Gestapo.

We have nothing done [sic] that was not our duty and the people who think that the Germans helped us to come in [sic] England, what I suppose they think, then they are mistaken.

I swear by the Mighty God, in whom I believe, that I am not guilty.

This, Sir, you can regard as my oath.

I want you to come in touch with H.M. the Queen and with the highest officers of the Intelligence Service. If this cannot help you, I ask you kindly to complain in the House of Lords.

I should like it very much to have an interview with you personal [sic]; if this is not possible, I ask you to use your influence to bring us in contact with Intelligence Officers and if this cannot be done, I want you to bring this matter before Court, where I can defend myself.

If the people, who ordered our arrest, think that it is better to separate us from the outside world, then there are places enough outside a prison, where I am between walls and bars and I consider it as hurting my feelings of honour to be in the same prison as deserters and criminals.

I ask you, Sir, respectfully but with the utmost pressure to do everything you can do to help us, as Dourlein and I are unable to do anything at all. I feel that I cannot live longer in these circumstances, and I fear to loose [sic] my mind very soon.

In the hope that you get cleared the matter quickly.

Colonel de Bruijne and Prince Bernhard approached the British authorities to release the two men, which eventually took place in June 1944. Gubbins, the man in overall charge of the SOE at the time, offered up his reasons for the way the two men were treated, which was more a justification rather than an apology. To make matters worse, once handed back to the Dutch authorities, they were downgraded rank wise by the Dutch Naval Command. Dourlein went from being a Sergeant to Corporal, whilst Ubbink was demoted from Lieutenant to Sergeant. Ubbink left the Dutch Royal Navy to become a steersman in the Merchant Navy. He survived the war and passed away on 31 March 1993, aged 71. As for Dourlein, he joined No. 320 (Netherlands) Squadron, RAF of the Naval Aviation Service, where he became an air gunner in a Lockheed Hudson. After the war he joined the Merchant Navy, where he continued working until 1968. He died on 31 May 1976 whilst on holiday in Loch Alsh, Scotland.

Herman Johannes Overes was born on 19 October 1908 in Amsterdam, but his family moved to South Africa when he was a young boy and it was there he was living before the outbreak of the war, working as a carpenter.

He became a member of the SOE on 15 July 1942, and whilst undergoing his basic training used the alias of Herman Oomen, with the code name of 'Keur'.

Reports from Overes' file were from his time spent at STS 24b, which was located at Glaschoille, near Mallaig, and STS 51, Dunham House, where he undertook parachute training at nearby RAF Ringway, near Manchester. His training also saw him spend time at STS 6, where SOE students began their initial training to become a qualified agent. STS 17 covered the art of sabotage, STS 31 security training, and STS 61 the packing of parachute containers.

12 August 1942 – Sergeant van Blankenstein
Small and sturdy chap, keen, comradely, and obliging. Very popular amongst the rest of the party. Sound character.

4 September 1942 – Unnamed Instructor
Is a small and sturdy chap, sympathetic and very comradely. Is rather talkative. Very popular with the other students, who are always making fun of his height; but though he is small he has shown guts. He is reliable, drinks moderately. Friend of No. 10; they always keep together.

These reports are from two different training locations and yet the first lines of each entry are nearly the same. Did the second instructor simply copy what the first one had written and then add a bit more? There is, of course, also no confirmation of the name of the student who is referred to as No. 10.

Overes was due to be parachuted into the Netherlands the day before he was actually dropped off, but the aircraft he was due to leave on had some kind of mechanical problem and the flight was cancelled. With the matter resolved, the aircraft left the following evening and this time Overes and Ubbink were dropped over the hamlet of Valkenheide, north of Leersum, where they were immediately arrested and taken prisoner.

Between 3 December 1942 and 27 November 1943, Overes was held with Ubbrink at Haaren before being transferred to the concentration camp at Rawicz. When and where Overes met his death is uncertain. The Dutch War Grave Foundation records that he was executed at Rawicz on 7 September 1944. Most deaths of agents that took place at Rawicz did so in April 1944, whilst 7 September 1944 was one of the two days captured SOE agents were murdered at Mauthausen. His name does not appear on the memorial plaque at Mauthausen as one of the SOE agents who was murdered there, yet the Dutch National Archives shows him as having died there on 7 September 1944.

On 2 May 1953 Overes was posthumously awarded the Bronze Cross by the government of the Netherlands for his wartime bravery.

CHAPTER SEVEN

Agents Captured During Operation North Pole - 1943

The following agents were dropped into the Netherlands during the early months of 1943, before the flights were stopped by the RAF in May of that year. Operation North Pole officially came to an end on 1 April 1944, when Hermann Giskes sent his clear and unencrypted message to the SOE in London, thanking them for sending agents to the Netherlands over the previous years.

13 February 1943

Beatrice Wilhelmina Marie Albertina 'Trix' Terwindt was born in Arnhem on 27 February 1911, into a relatively wealthy and affluent family. Her mother, Albertina, was from French nobility, whilst her father, Constant, ran a business as a stone manufacturer. Despite being one of seven children, the family had sufficient funds for Trix to attend the prestigious Arnhem Boarding School for girls, the Sacré Coeur.

Despite her privileged education, Terwindt ultimately decided she wanted to become an air hostess, and in 1937 began her training with the Dutch national airline, KLM, as part of the very first batch of students.

After the Netherlands was occupied by German forces in May 1940, KLM operations effectively came to a halt. Despite there being no work, Terwindt was still paid her wages by the company. It was sometime during the summer months of 1941 that she first came into contact with members of the Dutch resistance movement, for whom she agreed to work. In March 1942 she was given the task of taking a Dutch cadet officer from the Netherlands to neutral Switzerland. She had no intention of sitting out the rest of the war, however, and so, via France, Spain and Portugal, she made her way to England where she arrived on 26 August and was awarded the Dutch Cross of Merit by Queen Wilhelmina.

It was whilst in London that Terwindt was first approached by Captain Airey Neave, who worked for British military intelligence and was in charge of organising escape routes throughout German-occupied Europe for Allied pilots shot down behind enemy lines, and to help get them safely back to Britain.

Terwindt is an interesting case, because although she is included as one of the Operation North Pole agents, in reality she was not. She did not even work for the SOE, but for MI9, and was not actually parachuted into the Netherlands in response to a request for more agents after one of the German-initiated messages that were sent to London by the use of a captured British wireless set.

How exactly Neave became aware of Terwindt is unclear, but he approached her to see if she would be interested in helping him set up the escape routes in the Netherlands. He explained that to do this she would need to return to her homeland, and despite the inherent dangers, she readily agreed. She was given the pseudonym Beatrice Thompson and the code name 'Chicory'.

Like all agents, regardless of what branch of military intelligence they worked for, Terwindt first had to undergo training to enable her to successfully undertake her work in the Netherlands. After she had successfully completed her training, she left England late in the evening of 13 February 1943 and was dropped by parachute at Kallenkote, in the early hours of 14 February. Rather than be met by elements of the local resistance movement, it was members of Germany's feared Gestapo who were waiting for her. It was a trap, and she had landed right in the middle of it.

What followed was a long and harrowing interrogation that continued for more than three days. She had clearly been trained well as she gave nothing away and betrayed nobody in the process. Whatever it was she said to her captors must have been relatively convincing, however, because despite the length of her interrogation, as far as is known she was not tortured.

It has been suggested that the only reason she was captured was because she just happened to have been parachuted into the Netherlands from the same aircraft that was carrying two SOE agents who were part of Operation North Pole. There is a problem with this assumption, however, as records show she was dropped into the Netherlands by parachute on 14 February, while the nearest date recorded as to a delivery of SOE agents was three days later, on 17 February, when three male agents were dropped from the skies above. The men in question, Klaas van de Bor, Cornelis Eliza van Hulsteijn, and Cornelis Carel Braggaar, were all immediately arrested just after they landed by members of the Gestapo, who once again were aware of the time and location of their arrival.

So, if Terwindt was parachuted into the Netherlands on her own, how did the Germans know the time and date she was coming, and where she was due to be dropped off if she was not a member of the SOE? Does this suggest the reason they knew Terwindt was on her way was because there was a German spy working high up in British military intelligence?

After having been held at the local Gestapo headquarters, Terwindt was sent to Haaren and held there with other North Pole agents exclusively on the second floor of the building. The first of these agents to be detained there had arrived in May 1942.

While conditions at Haaren and the treatment of those held there was much better than could have been expected (it was certainly far better than a German concentration camp or a POW camp), Terwindt found life there extremely difficult to cope with due to a combination of being held in solitary confinement and the idleness which came with having no mental stimulation or anything productive to keep herself occupied.

With the end of Operation North Pole in April 1944, Terwindt, along with other captured agents was moved from Haaren to the Oranjehotel prison in Scheveningen, where she arrived on 8 May.

On her arrival at Scheveningen, Terwindt was interviewed by Joseph Schreider, the head of Department 4E, of German counterintelligence, better known as the Abwehr, and a central figure of Operation North Pole. Two days later, Terwindt was transferred by train to the Ravensbrück women's concentration camp 90 km north of Berlin, where she remained until February the following year when she was transferred to Mauthausen. Despite her deteriorating health, she survived and was still in the camp when it was liberated by American forces on 5 May 1945. The Red Cross took Terwindt to St. Gallen in Switzerland, where she received much needed medical attention. She had been so physically weakened by her ordeal and time spent at both Ravensbrück and Mauthausen that it was six weeks before she was able to walk.

Terwindt was one of a small number of agents captured during Operation North Pole who survived the war. Afterwards, she was approached by KLM to set up and train the next generation of the company's flight attendants, a role she readily accepted. She was also asked personally by Queen Wilhelmina to become her lady-in-waiting, but despite her pride in such a consideration, it was an opportunity she graciously declined, believing it to be a position that was above her social standing in Dutch society.

Sadly, Terwindt's health never fully recovered from her time incarcerated at Ravensbrück and Mauthausen, and in 1949 she had to step down from her position with KLM, but she did not stay idle. In 1951 she wrote and published a book entitled *Een vrouw vloog mee* (A Woman Flew Along), which documented her experiences as a flight attendant with KLM. The same year she took the decision to emigrate to Canada, but it was a decision that was destined not to last that long, and by the end of 1952, she was back living in the Netherlands.

In addition to her award of the Cross of Merit, she also received the Bronze Cross (Netherlands) and the American Medal of Freedom, established by President Harry S. Truman to honour civilians, of any nation, whose actions aided in the war efforts of the United States or her allies.

16 February 1943

Three more SOE agents, Klaas van de Bor, Cornelis Eliza van Hulsteijn and Cornelis Carel Braggaar were dropped into the

Netherlands in the early hours of 17 February 1943. They landed at IJsselmeer and were immediately arrested by the German reception committee who had been patiently waiting for them.

Klaas van de Bor was born on 24 May 1913 in Barneveld, and before the outbreak of the war worked as an electric cable engineer. Having first arrived in England on 14 July 1942, he was extensively interrogated over the course of two days by unnamed members of MI6. In an attempt to not only prove who he was, but also to prove he was not working for the Germans, he provided the names and details of men he knew to be members of the Terschuur, Lunteren, Achterberg, Voorthuizeh and Barneveld Dutch resistance groups. This included the home addresses of these individuals, what they did for a living, how old they were, their height, hair and eye colour, whether they wore glasses, and whether they were married.

Having satisfied British military intelligence that he was not a German spy, van de Bor enlisted in the SOE and commenced his training on 24 September 1942 at STS 6. The first two reports on van de Bor help provide a flavour of the training staff's early opinion of him, or at least those of their author, Sergeant van Blankenstein.

2 October 1942
Has only been two months in this country and speaks hardly any English. He is fairly intelligent but slow in everything. Good humoured chap, sensible and talkative.
9 October 1942
Is a simple and good natured man, who has NOT had a very good education. This sometime slightly handicaps him, but he is intelligent and makes up for it by his keenness and good will.

Compare these two reports to the next one, written just three weeks later on 30 October by the same man: 'Physically and mentally gross and unrefined. He even shocks his commander by his lack of good manners and of elementary politeness. Good hearted and even tempered. He is also determined and courageous.'

Not only is it vastly different from the first two reports, but the opening lines paint a horrendous picture of van de Bor when compared to the latter ones. In the Netherlands he was a wanted man for the murder of a German Gestapo officer and his fellow trainee agents had told him that they did not want to work with him. The Gestapo officer murdered by van de Bor in Ranswoude was Lieutenant Helmet Wetsko. The reason he was murdered was because he had provided a story to van de Bor pretending to be a downed German pilot who had had enough of the Nazis and wanted to make his way to England. The report continued.

> He has a vivid imagination; whatever adventure or incident is related to him; he invariably and immediately can tell you something along the same lines that has happened to him.
>
> A serious illness (typhus), which he contracted in France, has affected his heart; he has difficulties in breathing when he has to do arduous exercise.

When reading the information about van de Bor from 30 October onwards, it is staggering how he was accepted as an SOE agent for undercover work. Besides the disparaging remarks made about him by Sergeant van Blankenstein, it also has to be remembered that van de Bor was wanted for the murder; not something that would have been forgotten about, or easily forgiven. With that in mind, how is it possible for anybody to believe it would have been a sensible idea to send him back to the Netherlands, for any reason at all? If he was captured and his identity as a wanted man was discovered, the chances were that his death would have been neither swift nor pleasant.

Cornelis Eliza 'Kees' van Hulsteijn (Hulsteyn) was born on 8 February 1912 in Terneuzen. Before the war he worked as an architect in Johannesburg, South Africa, and had arrived in England in May 1940, enlisting in the SOE the following July. For the duration of his course he used the name of Kees van der Hoorn, and was allocated the code name of 'Otten'.

Included in van Hulsteijn's SOE file are a number of reports, including one by Sergeant van Blankenstein, dated 4 September 1942.

> This student was on his way to Holland when the invasion of the Low Countries started. He had to change his course and come to England. In the Dutch Brigade, where he enlisted

as a volunteer, he was the platoon Sergeant of some of the students. He is intelligent, keen and likes responsibilities. He likes a drink but does not drink immoderately. Was unable to do Lumbago training because of a weak knee. Is security minded.

Van Hulsteijn was posthumously awarded the Dutch Bronze Cross on 2 May 1953 for his war time exploits.

Along with his two colleagues, Cornelis Carel Braggaar was dropped at IJsselmeer on 17 February. Prior to the outbreak of the war, he had worked as an officer in the Dutch Merchant Navy on board merchant vessels operating out of the port of Amsterdam. He also had the added skill of being a qualified wireless operator.

He enlisted in the SOE on 23 June 1942. Whilst undergoing his training, he used the alias name of Cornelis Carel van Bakel. Braggaar was considered to be a 'reliable chap' who was well-liked by his fellow students, although he struggled in social settings when in the company of his colleagues, which was the main downside to his shyness. He was, however, 'an admirer of the fair sex' and got on with them very well, according to one of his instructors, Corporal Boks. This is despite the fact that he was engaged to Ada van Hemet, the sister of fellow SOE agent Jerry van Hermert.

After successfully passing his course, he also used the alias of Pieter van Veen and his code name was 'Bert'. After his arrest and incarceration, he died on 6 September 1944 at Mauthausen.

18 February 1943

Two days after the previous flight had left England, on 18 February SOE agents Gerrit van Os, Jan Christiaan Kist, Pieter van der Wilden and his cousin Willem van der Wilden were dropped by parachute near Voorthuizen and immediately arrested by a waiting German reception committee.

Gerrit van Os was born on 2 May 1914 in Hilversum. He attended primary school in his hometown until he was 8, before the family moved homes to nearby Naarden-Bussum and then again to Bloemendaal, where he completed his elementary schooling aged 16.

He then moved away from home and went to live in Amsterdam whilst he attended technical college, but when he was 18 had to return home to take over his father's garage due to an illness which prevented him from being able to carry on working.

In September 1934, having turned 20, he was called up for military service and was attached to the Dutch Air Force, but after he had completed his mandatory twelve months of service, he decided to remain in the Air Force and qualify as a pilot, eventually receiving his wings on 14 May 1936. It was through this work that he became involved in intelligence work in the Netherlands.

After the Dutch capitulation, van Os and others were tasked with flying to different locations throughout the Netherlands to collect property from the various flying grounds. It was because of this work that he was able to collect and collate relevant information about the locations, movement and numbers of German troops and vehicles. He was also able to collect and hide such items as firearms, ammunition and medical supplies. As time went on and the German occupation continued, it became obvious to van Os that he could be of more use in the fight against the Nazis by making his way to England. After a long and tiring journey, which saw him travel through Belgium, France and Spain, he arrived at Gourock on the west coast of Scotland on 31 July 1942.

An individual by the name of R.S. Sands, the member of British military intelligence who interrogated Os, says in his report dated 14 August 1942: 'He may be inclined to exaggerate, and he may be actually rather dumb, but I cannot find any grounds for regarding him as anything else than a good patriot. In the circumstances I do not see any danger in releasing VAN OS for incorporation in the Dutch Forces and I have every confidence in recommending this.'

Another report contained within van Os' SOE file, dated 21 September 1942, provides more information about his journey to Britain (note the slight difference in spelling of his surname):

As I informed you by telephone this afternoon, Lt Gerard VAN OSS [sic] first came to our notice in March 1942 when our representative in Geneva informed us that VAN OSS, who claimed to be a British secret agent known as "L.X.24", had reached Toulouse, together with George Albert VAN DAM MERRETT who claimed his father worked in the Admiralty in London, and LT. Joannes Henri KNOOP of the Dutch Colonial Army. From the answer to this telegram sent to Geneva, it would appear that the Dutch knew these men, but that we considered VAN OSS suspect and the other two indiscreet, at the same time advising our representatives in Geneva that his organisation in unoccupied France should not facilitate their journey to Spain.

In June 1942 we advised D.P.C. who had in the meantime received a visa application for VAN OSS, that we had no reason to consider this man as being suspect and an agent provocateur. It would appear that this trace did not prevent VAN OSS from being issued with a visa and coming to this country. When he passed through the Patriotic Schools on 13 August 1942, the MI5 examiner was favourably impressed by this man and could find no grounds for regarding him as anything else but a good patriot.

From the above you will see that the reports on VAN OSS are very conflicting, but from the telegrams we sent to our representative in Geneva in March 1942 there must have been some reason for suspecting this man, although there appears to be no trace to his detriment, and I think we should inform SO2 that we would not recommend him as a prospective agent.

To add to the confusion and uncertainty surrounding van Os, a note on his SOE file dated just two days later, 23 September, declared: 'Note from Netherlands Security Department certifying that Sgt. Pilot Gerard VAN OS, RNAF, is considered to be a trust worthy and faithful Dutch subject.'

Having arrived in England, van Os enlisted in the SOE on 24 September and whilst undergoing training used the alias surname of van Oosterom.

The morning after he was arrested, van Os was taken to the prison camp at Haaren, where for some reason his surname was recorded as being Oostveen. From Haaren he was transferred to the Rawicz prison camp in April 1944, and was known to have still been there in July 1944. Along with a number of other Dutch SOE agents, he was later transferred to the concentration camp at Mauthausen, where he was one of those killed on 6 September 1944. On 2 May 1953 he was posthumously awarded the Bronze Cross by the government of the Netherlands.

Jan Christiaan Kist was born on 22 September 1912 in Leiden, and from 1937 to 1938 attended the Artillery Reserve Officer's School in Utrecht, after which time he returned to studying law until 28 August 1939, when he was mobilised. Just four months later he was granted leave to continue his studies, but this in turn was cancelled on 7 May 1940 when he was sent to the Mechanised Artillery Depot near Leiden, where he was demobilised just eighteen days later on 25 May. He then continued his studies at Leiden until the end of November 1940, when the university was closed. He became a teacher of classical languages at a private boarding school, whilst at the same time working as the assistant librarian at Leiden; positions he remained in until the school closed for the summer holidays in August 1941.

Wanting to be part of the fight to rid his country of the scourge of Nazi Germany, Kist decided the best way to do this was by making his way to England where he could hopefully enlist in the British Army. Along with some friends, he took the decision to put his plan into action and on 23 September 1941, the journey to England began with a train journey from Leiden to Roosendaal. The following days and weeks saw them travelling by train, bus and on foot through Belgium and France, doing their best to avoid coming into contact with either members of the local police or German soldiers. By 7 October, Kist and his friend Hans Battarrd, a fellow student from Leiden, had reached the French city of Lyon. From here the two men made their way into Spain and from there it was on to Gibraltar.

Kist finally arrived in Britain, alongside Gerrit van Os, on 31 July 1942. On 1 October he was awarded the Dutch Cross of Merit by the Dutch government in exile in London, the citation of which read as follows: 'For having prepared his escape with great tact from enemy occupied Holland having executed his escape and voyage to

England courageously and tactfully in a situation of great danger due to enemy action.'

On his SOE file is a brief, unauthored report dated 14 December 1942:

> Application is made hereby for this student to attend a course at B area schools commencing on 16 December 1942. This man is intended for special work which does not necessitate his being trained in demolitions. For this reason he has not been sent to a para-military school.

Enlisting in the SOE on 11 November 1942, during his training he used the alias of Jan Christiaan Karels. Along with Gerrit van Os, he was captured on landing near Voorthuizen on 19 February 1943.

It is unclear with any degree of certainty where, when or how Kist actually died. Initially he was taken to the old seminary prison camp at Haaren, where he remained until the end of 1943 before being transferred to Rawicz. It is possible that he died in April 1944, as it is known that other SOE agents met their death at the camp at or around the same time. After the war, Kist was posthumously awarded the Bronze Cross in October 1953.

Pieter and Willem van der Wilden were also dropped by parachute near Voorthuizen on 18 February, although it is unclear as to whether they jumped from the same aircraft and at the same time as Os and Kist.

Pieter van der Wilden was born on 8 May 1914 in Haarlem, while his cousin Willem was born on 1 June 1910 in Hilegom.

In the years before the war, Pieter and Willem went to stay in South Africa, where they worked as bricklayers and construction workers. Whilst there they met fellow Dutchman Frederik Willem 'Freek' Rouwerd in Pretoria. When the war broke out and the Netherlands was later occupied, the three men decided they had to try to help their country in its hour of need, and the best way they felt they could do this was to make their way to Britain and join the fight against ridding their country of its unwelcome invaders.

With the Dutch government in exile in London, the three men had plenty of options to choose from as to how they could best join the fight as part of the Allied cause. For Pieter van der Wilden, this meant becoming a temporary conscript sergeant at the Special Assignments Bureau (BBO), which was a Dutch secret service established during the Second World War by the Dutch government in London. Its purpose was to arrange the deployment of agents, mainly Dutch exiles, to be returned to the Netherlands to assist local resistance groups, similar to the SOE.

Pieter enlisted in the SOE on 15 July 1942, and whilst on his course used the alias surname of Wouters. Later he also used the alias of Pieter van der Berg. The first report about him recorded on his SOE file, which was compiled during his period of training, was written on 12 August 1942 by one of his instructors, Sergeant van Blankenstein. It was extremely brief, direct and to the point: 'Intelligent but a bit slow. No initiative.'

The same instructor later wrote another report on Pieter dated 4 September 1942: 'Very placid. Has not got a very strong will and sometimes lacks confidence in himself. He often has to be persuaded that he can do a thing, for which he has declared himself incapable of doing, before even trying. I can speak highly of his morale and character. He is also security minded.'

Willem van der Wilden also enlisted in the SOE on 15 July 1942, and whilst undergoing his training used the alias name of Willem van der Western.

Willem was a married man whose wife lived in Pretoria, South Africa, and remained there after her husband had made his way to England. It was an extremely difficult decision for him to leave his wife behind, but with all the uncertainty of what was going on in Europe, and more importantly what might end up happening, it was the safest and most sensible option.

One of his instructors, Sergeant van Blankenstein, wrote a number of reports about him during his weeks of training. The first of these was dated 12 August 1942: 'Comic of the party. Always joking and wisecracking. Intelligent, quick and reliable and security minded. Was associated with No. 6 in South Africa.'

No. 6 was a reference to Frederik Willem 'Freek' Rouwerd, whom Willem and Pieter had met whilst working in Pretoria. The next report was dated 4 September 1942:

Cousin of No. 9 [Pieter van der Wilden]. He was a carpenter before the war and was associated with No. 6. Very sensible, and a reliable man. Good humoured and very popular. Has a strong personality. Learns easily and is quick minded. When off duty likes to have a good time. Entirely trustworthy on security grounds.

When they were initially detained following their capture on 18 February, the two cousins were taken to the prison camp at Haaren before later being transferred to Rawicz. They ended up at Mauthausen where they were killed on 6 September 1944. The names of both men are recorded on the plaque that was later erected at the camp.

10 March 1943

This was the night that Pieter Dourlein, Pieter Cornelis Boogaart and Pieter Arnoldus Arendse were dropped into the Netherlands by parachute near Ermelo and immediately arrested by German forces. Most of Dourlein's story in relation to his escape from Haaren, his journey back to England, and his subsequent arrest and incarceration in a London prison, is included in the story of Johan Bernard Ubbink, which is recorded earlier in this book (see 29 November 1942), so below are further details about his original escape from the Netherlands and how he made his way to England.

Dourlein was born on 2 February 1918 in the city of Veere. When he was 16 years of age he enlisted in the Dutch Royal Navy until being placed on the 'Reserve' in May 1940, and remained at home until briefly becoming a police officer between January and May 1941.

His story begins long before his deployment to the Netherlands and arrest on landing. On 11 June 1941, Dourlein, along with Jan Adrianus den Ouden, and K. de Korver, acquired a motorboat and made their way towards England, but two days later they still had not completed the journey. Eventually the three men were picked up by a Royal Navy minesweeper and taken to the port of Sheerness. All three men were awarded the Bronze Cross by the Dutch government in exile in London.

After having been interrogated by British military intelligence, he continued his military service in the Dutch Royal Navy and served aboard the Gerard Callenburgh-class destroyer HNLMS *Isaac Sweers*, seeing a great deal of action over the next year or so. He enlisted in the SOE on 24 September 1942 and just seven weeks later, on 13 November, the *Isaac Sweers* was attacked by the German submarine *U-431* and sunk after being hit by two torpedoes. Out of a crew of 194 officers and men, 108 were killed.

The SOE file on Dourlein, whose alias while he was training was Pieter Diepenbroek, includes a number of reports by members of the training staff. One of these is dated 30 October 1942:

Is most intelligent; has a strong will, is stubborn and determined. He was in the Dutch 'Marechaussee Police Force', when he decided to escape to England in a small motorboat. He has shown me a diary which relates his adventures from the invasion day till his departure of the Dutch destroyer on which he served over here. The escape itself is described in detail and the whole story reveals the man's character, self determination and audacity.

Physically a lean, strong and tough man, very handy and adaptable to any kind of work. He is intelligent, has not had much education, is quick on the uptake. He is very stubborn and has a violent temper. When in his normal mood, he is most reasonable, quiet, almost shy, but when angered he seems to lose some of his self-control. He is fond of drink and likes going out and having a good time. His violent temper never lasts long and should NOT be taken seriously. He is definitely suited to this kind of work.

When he arrived in Spain during his escape from Haaren, he was asked to write a report for the Dutch Embassy in Madrid, which he did. This report was extremely detailed and included details to his time in prison:

On or about the 20th April 1943 Boogaart and I succeeded in contacting the prisoners below us who smuggled messages outside in some way or other. We then passed on the following message for England. 'All agents arrested, entire organisation in German hands already for months owing to treason.' On or about the 14th May 1943, we received the following reply. 'Your message received in London, the matter will be investigated.

After initially being detained in Brixton prison in London on his return to England, he was released to the SOE's training station, STS 28 at Tyting House, Guildford. Although he was no longer incarcerated, he was not totally free either. Whilst at STS 28, a number of reports were written about him, with on in particular, dated 13 May 1944, showing the lengths people held against their will can go to in an attempt to amuse themselves, whilst at the same time trying to aggravate those tasked with guarding them:

Has started a campaign of petty annoyance. This consists of going into the greenhouse with Ubbink, whilst thinking themselves unobserved, and planting seeds in amongst those already planted of a different variety. Also, of mating the various doe rabbits with the buck, in order, it is presumed, to upset the Government here. It does nothing more than upset the rabbits. Apart from these childish tricks, he has been very quiet since his interview on 6 May 1944.

With the examination of his story of escaping from Haaren completed, he was released from STS 28 on the morning of 27 May 1944.

By the end of the war Dorlein was a gunner with No. 320 Dutch Squadron RAF, which was part of the Naval Aviation Service. He died on 31 May 1976 whilst on holiday in Loch Alsh, Scotland. He was 58. Originally the SOE file on Dourlein, held at the British National Archives was not due to be released for public consumption until 1 January 2024, but this was brought forward and took place in June 2009.

Pieter Cornelis Boogaart was born on 10 August 1918 in Graauw. He enlisted in the SOE on 24 September 1942 and during his weeks of training used the alias of Pieter Cornelis Bleeker, with the code name of 'Herman'. Sergeant van Blankenstein made the following observations in a report dated 2 October 1942:

> Sympathetic and intelligent man, good natured and very comradely. Understands English and speaks it a little. Seems very conscientious and willing to do his best. Has recently been decorated with the Order of Oranje-Nassau for his work in the Navy, where he has served for 11 years. Likes to talk of his adventures at sea in a quiet and simple way. Has strong patriotic feelings; he told me that he joined this organisation because he felt that he be of greater value to his country in this way.

Nearly two months later, van Blankenstein's opinion of Boogaart had changed somewhat, with his report dated 21 November 1942 including the following:

> Physically tough and mentally strong minded. He is very outspoken, says exactly what he thinks about everything and everybody and is generally a good judge in the matter. He knows his own value and is therefore slightly conceited. He likes you to feel that he is the best man. He is a good drinker and is fond of the women and having a good time. But this is done on the quiet, very security minded.

Is this because Boogaart had changed his attitude or had simply become more comfortable in his new surroundings and with the people he was with, or was it more a case of the instructor seeing him in a different light? By way of example, what he originally saw as positivity with a good attitude, he later saw as arrogance.

It is known that after his capture Boogaart was initially held at the old seminary at Haaren and was later transferred to Rawicz, where a report contained in his SOE file states he was last seen alive there in July 1944. He was later moved to Mauthausen, where the date of his death is believed to have been 7 September.

Pieter Arnoldus Arendse was born on 14 February 1912 in The Hague, and, after finishing his education, earned his living working as a carpenter. He married Berandina Versteegt in South Africa in 1937, but after she died in 1940, he returned to the Netherlands and from there made his way to England.

Arendse enlisted in the SOE on 15 July 1942, but during his training he used the surname of Dirk. At first sight he was not an obvious choice for life as a secret agent. In fact, he was quite the opposite. He was 6 feet 1 inches tall, with dark blond hair, and wore glasses that did not hide his 'rather staring eyes'. He also had large, slightly protruding teeth; certainly not ideal if you wanted to blend into the crowd.

Sergeant van Blankenstein wrote the following report about Arendse on 4 September 1942:

> Is a gifted and reliable man. He is intelligent, understands everything quickly and is very keen. He was a sergeant in the Dutch Army when he did his military training before the war. Is security minded and can be trusted. He has shown a great deal of initiative during the whole course. He likes responsibility and jobs where he can display his knowledge. He drinks little and keeps a quiet and reserved attitude when he is out.

It is known that Arendse was at Rawicz prison camp in July 1944, as he was seen and recognised by an unknown French agent who escaped from the camp in July 1944. He died at Mauthausen on 7 September 1944.

21 April 1943

Three agents were dropped into the Netherlands on this date and were immediately arrested. Antonius Johannes 'Klaas' Wegner, landed at IJsselmeer, whilst Frederik Rouwerd and Ivo van Uytvanck were dropped near the Dutch village of Garderen.

Antonius Johannes 'Klaas' Wegner was born on 20 September 1915 in Leiden. He was only 8 old when his parents, Antonius and Aagtje, divorced. Both parents subsequently married again, with Antonius deciding to live with his mother and stepfather, Willem

Sabee. Antonius Senior married Elisabeth Gruber, but after this he saw little of his son.

Initially Antonius decided on a life at sea, and in 1929, when he was still only 14, he began training as a sailor at the Merchant Navy training school in Rotterdam. In the following years he continued his naval training, but in 1935 he left and became a member of the Guards Regiment Grenadiers and Hunters, an infantry regiment of the Dutch Army. By August 1941, his nation having capitulated to the Germans and his days as a soldier in the Dutch Army behind him, he decided he both wanted and needed to do something to help free his country. Along with three of his trusted friends, he began his journey to freedom.

The four men made their way to Barcelona via Belgium, France and Switzerland. Once there, Wegner visited the Dutch consulate which directly led to him and Jacob Ruys, one of his travelling companions, boarding the SS *Isla Tenerife* and making their way to Gibraltar, where they arrived on 2 November 1941. From there they boarded the MS *Batory*, a large ocean-going liner and arrived at Gourock, Scotland on 8 January 1942.

On 24 January, two weeks after his arrival, Wegner was in London being interviewed by Oreste Pinto, a Dutch National who worked for MI5 at the Patriotic School in Wandsworth. It was here that incoming refugees to Britain were interrogated to determine whether they were genuine refugees or German spies. Happy with his story, Pinto passed Wegner as a genuine refugee and he enlisted in the SOE on 23 March 1942. During his training he used the alias of Antonius de Kluif.

Not all the reports included in his SOE file are positive. For example, a typed report headed simply 'DE KLUIF' (Wegner's alias used whilst training), and dated in pencil 27 July 1942, mentioned how the author had received a letter from four SOE students, Frank, Dubois, van Krimpen and Felders, who wanted to talk with him 'regarding the student DE KLUIF'. At the time of writing their letter, the four men were at STS 17 at Brickendonbury Manor in Hertfordshire, where sabotage training was taught. The author of the report went to see them and was somewhat surprised to hear that they all had 'very grave doubts as to the suitability of DE KLUIF for the field'.

Having worked alongside and lived with him for nearly four months, the men had come to the conclusion that he was unreliable, and would be a danger to them on a personal level and to the organisation as a whole. They were so concerned that they told the author not only did they not want to be associated with Wegner in the field, but that they would not be prepared to become active agents if they knew he would be sent as well. The author was unsurprisingly shocked by the comments the four men had made, but as so many had aired the same views, he took them seriously.

The author's report also included some of his own observations on the matter:

> The various reports on DE KLUIF, whilst not exactly glowing, have not been unfavourable and there is no suggestion that he is in any sense a 'wrong un' or liable, wittingly, to disclose information which should be kept to himself.
>
> I have by no means given up all hope of using DE KLUIF at a later date when his present companions have disappeared entirely, and provided that he has overcome that tendency to absent mindedness which is his most serious fault.

With the benefit of hindsight, it is quite surprising that a man who inspired so much doubt and concern as to whether he could effectively do his job sufficiently, was actually sent to the Netherlands. It could be interpreted that those in a position of authority within the Dutch section of the SOE were prepared to send anyone into the field, regardless of their overall suitability to be able to carry out the work they had been trained to do.

The Commandant of STS 51, the parachute training school, wrote a report dated 3 October 1942. In it he bemoaned the fact that Wegner 'arrived in a terribly unfit condition', was 'a morose individual who showed no enthusiasm for the work', and who he doubted could do 'a serious job of work'.

However, despite all the concerns as to Wegener's suitability to be deployed as an SOE agent, the decision was eventually taken that he should be sent.

Frederik Willem 'Freek' Rouwerd was born on 31 May 1912 in The Hague, and after completing his education became a carpenter. Due to a lack of work in his homeland, however, in 1937 he decided to make his way to South Africa and start a new life. He quickly settled into his new life where he married and became a father. Despite his newfound responsibilities, he left for England in 1942 with the intention of helping to free his nation from the grip of Nazi occupation.

He enlisted in the SOE on 20 June 1942 and began his course three weeks later on 15 July. During his training to become an agent, he used the alias name of Frederik Willem Roeleveld.

Sergeant van Blankenstein said of him in a report of 4 September 1942: 'Tough and able but lacks enthusiasm. Can become quickly downhearted and discouraged. He is a good drinker but can be trusted. He seems rather keen on women.'

Two months before he left on his mission, Rouwerd wrote his mother a farewell letter on 21 March 1943. It was only to be given to her if he failed to return. The first paragraph of the letter was as follows:

I hereby send you my last greeting from this world. Unfortunately, they have no choice, mother. I hope you do not grieve too much, for it is not up to us, but him, who decides on the ups and downs of the world. Dear mother, first of all I would like to thank you for all that you have done for me. Never was anything too much for you, never was anything too heavy for you.

It would be harder to find a clearer indication that Rouwerd knew his was a mission he might not return from, but despite this he still consented to go. That is bravery beyond belief. A man accepting his fate and destiny but refusing to shy away from what he had to do, even though he knew in his heart it would ultimately cost him his life.

What eventually happened to Rouwerd remains a mystery. It is known that along with Wegner and van Uytvanck he was initially taken to the prison at Haaren, and that in July 1944 he was being held at Rawicz, but after this time it becomes a guessing game as to what actually happened.

Ivo van Uytvanck was born on 7 July 1917 at Bussum. He went to school in nearby Apeldoorn between 1931 and 1933, and then moved with his family to live in South Africa, where he continued his education at both high school and university up until 1937, before finding work as an assistant secretary.

Wanting to do his bit for his country, he travelled to England in early 1942, and after having been interrogated and cleared by British military intelligence, he enlisted in the SOE on 15 July 1942. Four months later, he married 22-year-old Heather Gwendoline Buchanan in Kensington, London. During his training to become an agent with the SOE, he used the alias name of Ivo van Unnik.

The SOE file on van Uytvanck was not originally supposed to have been released into the public domain until 1 January 2024, but this was subsequently brought forward to 1 July 2009.

One of the reports on him was written by Sergeant van Blankenstein and is dated 4 September 1942, when van Uytvanck was at STS 51 for parachute training at nearby RAF Ringway:

> The youngest member of the group, 6 feet 4 tall. Very intelligent, even tempered and pleasant, sympathetic, and slightly conceited. He likes to boast in a jolly way how well he can do certain things, and always gets his leg pulled by the others who make fun of him.
>
> He likes to enjoy himself and have a good time. Being good looking he has much success with the women, but he is quite unspoiled and does not seem very interested himself. I have had no problems with him security wise.

No matter how good a student he was, being a good-looking man who was 6 feet 4 inches tall with an athletic physique, and who attracted a lot of attention from women, did not make him an ideal candidate to work as a spy, quite the opposite, in fact.

After his capture he was held at a number of different locations, including the police station at Scheveningen, the prison camps at Haaren, Assen, Rawicz, and finally Mauthausen concentration camp, where he was killed on 7 September 1944. The records at Mauthausen give his prison number as 96508, and that his cause of death was, '*auf der flucht erschossen*'; shot when escaping.

21 May 1943

Late on the evening of this date, three SOE agents left England and were dropped by parachute near the Dutch village of Garderen in the early hours of the following morning, where they were immediately arrested. These men were Oskar Willem de Brey, Anton Mink, and Laurens Punt.

Although they were not the last British or Dutch agents sent to the Netherlands during the war, they were the last of the North Pole agents captured by the Germans before Hermann Giskes sent his now famous taunting message to the SOE hierarchy, which ended by promising a warm reception to any further agents the SOE might be considering sending to the Netherlands.

Oskar Willem de Brey was born on 1 October 1921. As a young boy he attended school in The Hague before going on to study aeronautical engineering at university in Delft. Alongside his studies he helped his fellow compatriots who wished to escape after Dutch military forces capitulated on 15 May 1940. His involvement in this work brought him to the attention of the Gestapo, which meant he had become a wanted man.

After a failed attempt to make their way to England via the North Sea in folding canoes, de Brey and his friend Pim de Bruyn Kops decided to try again in December 1941, but this time on foot. They made their way across the Netherlands, through Belgium, into France, and by August 1942, having crossed the Pyrenees mountains, arrived in Bilbao, Spain. From there they took a ship and made their way to the United States, and, four months later, having travelled on to Canada, the pair were in England, arriving on 17 December.

De Brey enlisted in the SOE on 18 January 1943 and soon began his training to qualify as an agent. One of the reports compiled about him, which is contained within his file, was written by Sergeant Mendes and is dated 18 February 1943:

Very determined to master all subjects and is exceptionally quick in doing so. His youth doesn't seem to handicap him. He has a deep sense of responsibility and good emotional self-control. Possesses the essential qualities of mind and mental alertness, combined with a cheerful disposition, resulting in a very sound character. His opinion regarding certain individuals and or situations, is normally highly valued by the others on his course.

During his training he used the alias of Oskar de Blank, and he was allocated the code name of 'Theo'. It is also noted on his file that he had a Jewish appearance. That being the case, it is not clear how he would have been deemed suitable to be sent to the German-occupied Netherlands following the census carried out by the Nazis in 1941 to establish the number of Jews living there. A total of 139,717 Dutch Jews were registered, the figure falling to around 35,000 by the end of the war.

De Brey was initially held with his two colleagues at Haaren, although it is unclear as for how long. He was subsequently moved to Mauthausen, where he was murdered on 7 September 1944. He had been awarded the Dutch Cross of Merit on 25 February 1943 by the Dutch government in exile, and after the war, on 2 May 1953, he was posthumously awarded the Bronze Cross and his nation's War Remembrance Cross.

Anton Berend Mink was born in Den Helder on 21 October 1918, and grew up in Nieuwediep. His father, Dirk, was a Sergeant in the Dutch Royal Navy, and it was in his father's footsteps that Anton wanted to follow. After having completed his education, his first job was as an apprentice working in a shipyard.

In May 1938 he began his National Service in the Army, most of which was spent as part of a coastal battery unit. Soon after Germany occupied the Netherlands in May 1940, he was demobilised and returned to civilian life, where he found work as a customs officer working at a number of locations throughout the country. Like the majority of his fellow Dutchmen, he was unhappy at his country being under the control of Nazi Germany. He had two choices: he could stay where he was and remain in his job as a customs officer in relative comfort and safety, or he could make his way to England, enlist in a branch of the British armed forces, and in doing so help speed up the process of freeing his country. He chose the latter. His journey to England began on 22 April 1942 when he crossed the border into Belgium and finished eight months later when he arrived in England from Canada on 18 December.

He enlisted in the SOE on 18 January 1943, and during his training used the alias of Anton Berend Mertens. Sergeant Mendes wrote the following report about him on 29 January:

> The most quiet of them all. Generally speaking, always agrees with the others but seldom raises a point himself; is more the regular, and in this case, quite intelligent soldier type. Temperate habits with regards women, drink etc.
>
> More than once during a conversation it transpires that there is a strong distrust or rather lack of confidence in their own authorities, should these be in command of operations. This is not merely an 'idee fixe' but is rightly or wrongly, based upon certain cases which have taken place in the past in their own country during the period they were still there, when, still according to them of course, the lack of organisation of their own countrymen have more than once been observed. Hence there is quite some anxiety as to under whose orders they are going to be placed.

The next report was written by Sergeant Mendes just three days later:

> Doesn't lack determination; tends however to be flustered in circumstances as for instance when working alone, without the protective guidance of others. I have asked myself the question whether this emotional instability might not handicap him under real trying operational circumstance.

It would have been a concern to the course instructors that they had noticed the above individual traits in Mink so early on in proceedings. The issue was whether to let him continue and hope that he would improve or cut their losses in the belief that there would be no improvement.

Mendes wrote another report on Mink dated 25 February 1943:

> His case still remains somewhat of a problem. Though he is an all round decent and charming fellow, he really doesn't possess any outstanding qualities. When chosen as leader he doesn't inspire confidence, but on the other hand he does not give cause to be mistrusted.
>
> Not possessing any outstanding personality, he remains perfectly inconspicuous amongst a crowd; and when told what to do, he will most likely manage to carry it out without question or argument, not because he has mastered the art of remining in the background, but merely because he is naturally so inclined.

Despite the real and present concerns of Sergeant Mendes and the rest of the SOE training staff about the effectiveness of deploying Mink in the field on a live operation, he passed the course and was deployed to the Netherlands just two months later.

This concern as to whether an individual student was going to make an effective agent was a common theme running through a number of the agents who completed their training and were then subsequently deployed to the Netherlands. Going by the notes made by the training staff, it could be rightly argued that some of these men were not 100 percent suited to the role they were asked to do and should have not been deployed on active service. That being the case, the obvious question this leads to is why were they then sent?

If there were concerns by the British that the Germans had somehow managed to infiltrate the SOE's operation, due to the arrests of Zomer, Schrage, van Hamel and Alblas, then perhaps there was no real concern about the overall capabilities of the men who were subsequently sent.

After his arrest, Mink and his two colleagues were initially held in custody at Haaren, before being moved to Rawicz, where he was still known to be alive as late as July 1944. At some point after that he was transferred to Mauthausen, where he was subsequently murdered on 7 September.

For escaping the Netherlands and making his way to England, Mink was awarded the Cross of Merit by the Dutch government in exile on 25 February 1943. On 2 May 1953, he was posthumously awarded the Bronze Cross for his time spent as an agent of the SOE.

Laurens Maria Punt was born on 13 October 1918 in Alkmaar into a deeply religious Roman Catholic family and was one of ten children born to Hendrikus and Catharina Punt. Some records also show his surname as being 'Point', but his SOE file only lists the name Punt.

After he had finished his education, he then spent the following twelve months working as a clerk in an office in Alkmaar, before enlisting in the Dutch Army on 31 March 1938. After he had successfully completed his basic training, he was allocated to the 21st Infantry Regiment and stationed in Amersfoort. On 6 May 1940, and by now a Sergeant, he was one of those deployed to help defend Den Helder against the invading German forces. On 26 June, after the Dutch government had capitulated, Punt, along with his colleagues, was demobilised and sent to Borkel en Schaff, in North Brabant, to work as a customs officer; a job he was unhappy with. Unlike his government, he was not so willing to capitulate. He wanted to continue the fight in any way that he could, and knew his best option was to try to make his way to England. The question he kept asking himself was how he would do it, but without any contacts, or anybody to help him along the way, the task was fraught with danger. He also had to be careful about whom he could trust. One wrong decision and he could quite easily end up in a German prison camp.

On 3 December 1941, Punt met three French POWs who had managed to escape from their incarceration at Osnabruck in Germany and arrive in Borkel en Schaft whilst trying to make their way back to France. This was the opportunity he had been waiting for. Not only did he decide to help them, but he also decided to join them. The following morning, the four men crossed the border into Belgium at the town of Neerpelt, and within a matter of days they had arrived in Paris. Fortunately, Punt was a remarkably strong-minded individual, and he eventually arrived in England on 13 December 1942, more than a year after he had begun his journey.

After being repeatedly interrogated by members of British military intelligence, he finally managed to satisfy them as to his true identity and his reasons for coming to England. He enlisted in the SOE on 14 January 1943, and during his training went by the alias of Laurentius Maria Pijnenburg and was given the code name of 'Simon'.

It is understandable that in the circumstances, the exact dates and locations of when and where Punt was held are open to debate, but it is known that he was initially held in custody at Haaren before being taken to Mauthausen, where he was murdered on 7 September.

Punt was awarded the Dutch Cross of Merit on 25 February 1943 for his escape from occupied Netherlands, and posthumously awarded the Bronze Cross on 5 February 1953 for his time spent as an agent of the SOE.

After Operation North Pole came to an end, at least 126 agents from SOE, MI6, and MI9, were dropped into different countries throughout occupied Europe. Of these, eight were SOE agents dropped into the Netherlands.

The last Dutch SOE agent sent to the Netherlands was Anton Marie Jacob 'Tom' Gehrels, who was dropped by parachute on the night of 23 April 1945, landing near Ter Aar. He was just 20 years of age. His mission was to make contact with local resistance groups and help organise acts of sabotage against German forces, who by then were in full retreat. This allowed the Dutch resistance movement to become more prominent and less concerned about the possibility of being discovered or captured, which in turn led to a marked increase in the number acts of sabotage carried out.

Gehrels survived the war and returned to his studies, graduating from the University of Leiden in 1951 with a degree in physics and astronomy. Soon after this he moved to America where he attended the University of Chicago and obtained a doctorate in astronomy and astrophysics in 1956. He went on to become a major name in the field of astronomy, even having the minor planet, '1777 Gehrels', named in his honour.

CHAPTER EIGHT

Anton van der Waals – Collaborator

Anton van der Waals was born on 11 October 1912 in Rotterdam and was the youngest of four children. He was seen by his parents as a relatively bright child and as he grew into his teens, it became clear that he had a technical mind, showing an interest in both the technical workings of radios, as well as the mechanics of motorbikes and engines. He badly wanted to start up his own repair company for both radios and vehicles, but the idea never quite became a reality.

In 1937, at the age of 25, he found work as an electrician for a company in Rotterdam, which resulted in him spending much of his time installing and maintaining the electrical systems on board submarines and surface vessels of the Royal Dutch Navy.

He was both clever and astute in equal amounts. His intelligence and personal drive pushed him not just to settle working for the electrical company who employed him, but to design and develop his own ideas. He came up with a new design for an internal combustion engine, along with an improved and more powerful radio. The problem was that he did not seem to mind who was willing to purchase his new ideas; he actively tried to sell the ideas to the Dutch resistance and when they showed no interest, he then went to the other extreme and tried to sell to both the German Army and the Dutch National Socialist Movement (DSB), who politically led towards the Nazi Party. When neither organisation wanted to progress matters, he even considered selling his inventions to the

Allies. Whether these designs were actually his or someone else's is something which has never been truly confirmed.

It was sometime in either late 1940 or early 1941 when van der Waals started to become a *Vertrauensmann*, or *V-mann*, somebody who hunted Jews in hiding, members of the resistance, or downed enemy pilots. They also worked as informants for the German secret police, the SD. Why he did this or when he first began is unclear, but he quickly came to the attention of Joseph Schreider, the man who worked alongside Hermann Giskes, who was in charge of German counterintelligence throughout the occupied Netherlands. The two men first met in the middle of April 1941, and the meeting resulted in van der Waals becoming a full time, paid employee of the SD.

In April 1941, Hans Bierhuijs was a member of a resistance group from the town of Heemstede, located in the province of North Holland. On the evening of 20 April, the resistance group decided to blow up a German train, but things did not quite go according to plan and the attempt failed. During the melee that followed, a German railway worker was shot and killed by Hans Bierhuijs. After the incident, two members of the group, Henk Schoenmaker and Willem Zietse were betrayed by van der Waals, a man they believed to be called De Wilde. During their interrogation they gave up the name of their fellow resistance member who had carried out the shooting, Hans Bierhuijs, who was then hunted down and located by van der Waals. Bierhuijs, his elder brother Joseph, and one other member of the group was executed at an area near Wassenaar, on 30 September 1941. When a member of the Dutch resistance was arrested and van der Waals was present, he would be handcuffed and arrested as well in an effort to maintain his creditability in the eyes of resistance members who believed he was one of them.

It was in about May 1941 when members of the Dutch resistance first began to suspect van der Waals of being an informant for the Germans, and matters were not helped when around about the same time, a member of the resistance movement, Jan Kwak, was arrested by the Gestapo. He was initially held at the local Orange Hotel before being transferred to the Waalsdorpervlakte at Meijendel in Wassenaar, near The Hague, where he was executed by firing squad on 12 February 1942. It is believed that information provided by van der Waals led directly to Kwak's arrest, and his subsequent execution.

Three individuals, Otto Verdoorn, Arij van der Meer (a businessman and wartime resistance fighter), and policeman Jan van den Ende, were so incensed by what had happened that they decided to kill van der Waals. Van den Ende had warned van der Meer about doing business with van der Waals as he strongly suspected him of collaborating with the Germans. Before the three men could carry out their plan, however, van den Ende was arrested by the Gestapo on 7 August 1941, which coincided with van der Waals becoming a less visible individual, possibly because he realised his secret had been discovered. Unbeknown to van der Waals, Verdoorn, van der Meer and van den Ende had made two failed attempts on his life and were planning a third for the evening of 7 August, the same day that van den Ende was arrested. One of those present when van den Ende was arrested was their potential victim, van der Waals. If van den Ende had any lingering doubts about exactly which side van der Waals was on, his own arrest would no doubt have confirmed any such feelings and simply confirmed his worst fears.

Despite knowing his reputation amongst certain resistance groups was far from being positive, and that if he was discovered in certain parts of the country he would have been killed, van der Waals carried on being an informant for the German authorities.

On one occasion, in January 1943, he met a man named Christian Corneille Dutilh, who was the founder of what was known as the Kees Resistance Group located in Amsterdam. Van der Waals had introduced himself to Dutilh as Anton de Wilde and told him that he had just arrived from England. But his story, although believed by Dutilh, was not believed by everyone in the resistance movement, and despite informing Dutilh of their concerns, he still remained in close touch with the man he knew as Anton de Wilde. Sadly for Dutilh, this was a decision which ultimately cost him his life. When the two men were at a meeting on 10 March, members of the local Gestapo arrived at the address and both men were arrested. What Dutilh did not know was that van der Waals' arrest was only to prevent his cover as a traitor from being blown. Dutilh was executed by firing squad on 24 February 1944.

By June 1943, the net really was closing in on van der Waals, and even he knew that if he carried on for much longer, his luck would most definitely run out. His final act of betrayal of his fellow countrymen was that of Allard Lambertus Oosterhuis, who was the leader of the resistance group, 't Zwaantje, which had been infiltrated by van der Waals. Several members of the group were arrested, and some were executed by firing squad in June 1944, although a number survived the war and were liberated from their captivity in April 1945.

Van der Waals' situation became so perilous that to help try to protect him, the SD in Rotterdam officially announced he had been assassinated by the Dutch resistance. They even went as far as to offer a reward for those responsible for his demise. The truth was, however, that he had left for Sweden in September 1943 to try to trace the remnants of Oosterhuis' escape route he had been running to Sweden and beyond. It turned out to be a fruitless trip and less than a month later, van der Waals returned to the Netherlands. Now no longer of any use to the SD because of his notoriety, he continued to be paid by them, living in the town of Loosdrecht under the name of H.J. van Veen. He remained there without any more apparent involvement in his chosen way of living, but once a traitor, always a traitor, as the sins of his past did not suddenly disappear because he no longer took part in such activities.

As the war was finally nearing its end, van der Waals moved to the village of Zuidlaren and handed himself over to elements of the First Canadian Army, who had begun liberating the peoples of the northern and western Netherlands, specifically north of the River Mass, which included the major cities of The Hague, Amsterdam and Rotterdam. The winter of 1944/45 had been particular severe for the Dutch people, with somewhere in the region of 20,000 civilians perishing, mainly due to a shortage of both food and fuel.

Rather than being imprisoned, van der Waals was handed over to the British, although it is unclear exactly when he provided his true identity and that he was, in fact, a traitor. Whatever the truth of the matter, he was then used by the British Secret Intelligence Service, MI6, in post-war Germany, with the most likely scenario being that he was helping to hunt down high-ranking and wanted members of the Nazi Party, especially those wanted in relation to war crimes. He was told to try to infiltrate groups that were part of what was known as the Werwolf movement, where German soldiers and civilians were to fight back against the Allies during the last months of the war using guerrilla tactics. The Dutch were understandably furious at the British decision to use van der Waals in such a way, especially as he was one of the most notorious Dutch traitors of the war.

Once the British no longer had a use for van der Waals, and with some political pressure having no doubt been applied by the Dutch government, he was collected from the internment camp in Germany where the British had been holding him and handed over in 1947. His trial began at the Special Court of Justice in The Hague in April 1948 and lasted through until 7 May, when he was found guilty and sentenced to death. His case had not been helped when one of the witnesses produced by the prosecution to give evidence against him was none other than his ex-employer, Joseph Schreider.

During his trial, van der Waals mentioned on more than one occasion that he had been acting on the orders of a British spy by the name of John Verhagen who had instructed him to go and work for the SD to gain information about German activities in the Netherlands.

Appeals by himself and members of his immediate family proved fruitless, and he was executed by firing squad on 26 January 1950, ironically on the Waalsdorpervlakte, a plain on the outskirts of The Hague – the same place where more than 250 Dutch civilians had been murdered by the Nazis during the occupation. More than thirty of these individuals were resistance fighters who had been betrayed by van der Waals.

On the night before his execution, van der Waals admitted that John Verhagen was fictitious, and that he alone was responsible for those whom he had betrayed to the SD.

Van der Waals was not the only Dutch traitor of the war. In total, thirty-four Dutch nationals who were known to have collaborated with the Germans were executed for their crimes in the years after the war, although there were undoubtedly many, many more who remined undiscovered.

CHAPTER NINE

RAF Tempsford

The majority of flights which took SOE agents across the English Channel to carry out their clandestine operations throughout occupied Europe, including many of those who took part in Operation North Pole, began their journeys from the somewhat secretive RAF air base at Tempsford, located just over 2 miles northeast of Sandy, Bedfordshire, and just 4 miles south of St. Neots in Cambridgeshire, which was also known as Gibraltar Farm.

It had been the brainchild of the Air Ministry and work began on the site in the summer months of 1940. Keeping such a project secret was never easy, especially in a time of war, when nearly everybody was on heightened alert for strange goings on, and as far as the general public were concerned, anybody new in their midst was potentially a foreign spy. This meant convincing locals that such a large strip of land was nothing more sinister than a working farm, when aircraft were taking off and landing there, was no easy task.

The reality was that two RAF squadrons were based there, No. 138 and No. 161. There was a structured method to the times and dates of the flights, which were based on the timings of the full moons so that the pilots had the best possible visibility. The flip side of that equation meant that the same aircraft were vulnerable to being sighted by the enemy gun batteries they flew over, or near, to their intended destination.

These two squadrons were part of what were known as the Royal Air Force Special Duties (SD) Service. This was a secret air service that was created specifically to provide air transport to support the resistance movements of nations occupied by Nazi Germany and its Axis partners. Parachute drop was the primary method by which the Special Duties units carried out their work. Flights flew to specific locations in countries throughout occupied Europe, including the Netherlands. By the end of the war, the Special Duties units had expanded their area of operations to the Far East.

The purpose of these two squadrons was to drop off SOE agents to their allocated destinations, along with arms, supplies and other related equipment. They sometimes also had to collect returning agents who had completed their missions, downed air crews who had come into the hands of the local resistance movements, as well as escaping foreign dignitaries such as members of royal families or politicians.

Prime Minister Winston Churchill was a driving force behind the idea of not surrendering to the Germans. He was, however, also a realist and knew that Britain and her Commonwealth allies could not defeat them all on their own. They needed help in the shape of resistance movements which operated in the countries throughout Europe that were under German occupation. Churchill was determined that one day British and Allied forces would once again return to Europe to rid the world of Nazi Germany and all that it stood for. Churchill also knew that such a proposition would not happen any time soon, so until that time arrived, freedom fighters and resistance groups within each of these sovereign countries would have to continue the fight from within, but to become, and remain, effective, they would need help, which is where the agents of the SOE came in.

To enable Churchill's dream to become a reality, the Special Operations Executive came into being on 22 July 1940, under the command of Hugh Dalton under the guise of the Ministry of Economic Warfare. For it to be as effective as possible, every attempt was made to keep the very existence of the SOE secret. To do this its actions were never referred to explicitly, and any reference to it in an official capacity would result in it being referred to by such titles as the Inter-Services Research Bureau, the Joint Technical Board, or the Special Training Schools Headquarters.

For this new organisation to be effective, they would need aircraft to get to their destination. Submarines were out of the question as the entire European coastline from the top of Norway all the way down to the southernmost part of France was either covered in barbed wire, mine fields or artillery batteries. The only way for the SOE agents to reach their destinations was by parachute. But rather than being met with open arms, the SOE found itself facing resistance from the very top of the RAF in the shape of Air Marshal Charles Portal, who believed that aircraft and their crews were a scarce enough commodity as it was, and they could be far better deployed defending the nation's skies from German bombing raids than they could ferrying spies and agents backwards and forwards across the English Channel or North Sea.

Thankfully, Churchill won the argument and the SOE was furnished with its much-needed aircraft to enable it to carry out its clandestine operations throughout Europe. Against its better wishes, the Air Ministry acquiesced to Churchill's demands, and the Special Duties Service Units came into being just a month after the SOE itself had been formed. Initially they were part of No. 11 Group Fighter Command, but in October 1940, this was changed to No. 3 Group.

There were two types of aircraft used for the operation. If weapons, supplies or agents were to be dropped by parachute then this was done using a converted Handley Page Halifax bomber, but if there was a need for an aircraft to land, then a Westland Lysander STOL was used. The Halifax had its maiden flight on 25 October 1939, before entering service with the RAF on 13 November 1940, and went on to play an important role within Bomber Command as part of its nighttime bombing raids on a number of major cities and industrial areas of Nazi Germany. Despite this, it was not an aircraft particularly liked by the Commanding Officer of Bomber Command, Arthur Harris, who described the Halifax as inferior to its rival, the Lancaster, mainly because of its smaller payload, although this was not an opinion that was shared by a number of the Halifax crews.

The Lysander was manufactured by Westland Aircraft, from Yeovil in Somerset. It had only come into use in 1936 and just ten years later was put out of service. The initials STOL stood for short take-off and landing, meaning it was ideal for such clandestine work, but it was also used as a daytime photographic reconnaissance and observation aircraft.

Despite its unusual appearance, the Lysander was equipped with fully automatic wing slats and slotted flaps and an aerodynamic tailplane and was chosen for production by the Air Ministry against competing aircraft of a similar design. A massive advantage that the Lysander had was its short take-off and landing abilities, an attribute that was greatly appreciated by the pilots who flew the aircraft, especially when it came to taking off from an isolated field in German-occupied Netherlands.

The men of No. 138 Squadron carried out the bulk of the supply and agent drops, whilst No. 161 Squadron, who used the much smaller and easier to manoeuvre Lysander aircraft, did the insertion and pick-up operations, which sometimes meant picking up an agent moments after having just dropped one off.

Secrecy was paramount. Not only did the ground crews who serviced and maintained the aircraft that formed the Special Duties service not know the real purpose of the squadrons they looked after at RAF Tempsford, information about the squadrons and their personnel remained a secret from the British public until the late 1970s.

The entire operation was a big ask. Although the end game was for the RAF to deliver SOE agents behind enemy lines throughout occupied Europe, potential landing sites had to be identified for occasions when aircraft needed to land to pick up agents and other Allied personnel for transportation back to Britain. This also required people on the ground who had to prepare the identified landing site for the aircraft to be able to land safely.

The unit's secrecy was problematic when it came to recruiting pilots. After all, the roles could hardly be advertised, and invites were usually by word of mouth. A pilot from the unit who had heard of another particular pilot they thought might be a suitable candidate would make the initial contact, but whoever was selected had to be a special breed of pilot; multi-faceted men who could think quickly on their feet and be adaptable in fast moving and ever-changing circumstances. Besides being excellent pilots, they also had to be good navigators, the latter skill being even more important than the first. All their flights would take place during the hours of darkness on the night of a full moon, and possibly in inclement weather, over enemy held territory, so the pilot had to able to find their way to a remote landing strip or a location they had never been to before. To assist the pilots in their pick-ups, the RAF's Photographic Reconnaissance Unit would fly over the proposed landing site and photograph it, so that the pilots could study them at their leisure and prepare themselves.

The reason for nearly all the flights taking place on the night of a full moon, was to aid the navigation of the pilots, whose job was made difficult enough by flying in the dark to a location they quite possibly had never been to before. The only problem with this was that there were only twelve full moons in a year. Consequently, between 28 August 1940 and 21 May 1943 there were a total of thirty-two full moons, with drops taking place on the following evenings:

1940
Monday, 16 September
Friday, 15 November
Saturday, 14 December
1941
Monday, 13 January
Wednesday, 12 February
Thursday, 13 March
Friday, 11 May
Monday, 9 June
Tuesday, 8 July
Thursday, 7 August
Friday, 5 September
Sunday, 5 October
Tuesday, 4 November
Wednesday, 3 December
1942
Friday, 2 January
Sunday, 1 February

Tuesday, 3 March
Wednesday, 1 April
Friday, 1 May
Saturday, 30 May
Sunday, 28 June
Monday, 27 July
Wednesday, 26 August
Thursday, 24 September
Saturday, 24 October
Sunday, 22 November
Tuesday, 22 December
1943
Thursday, 21 January
Saturday, 20 February
Sunday, 21 March
Tuesday, 20 April
Wednesday, 19 May

Regardless of what the intention may have been, only four agents were actually dropped on the night of a full moon, and that was on 24 September 1942, when Karel Beukema toe Water, Kees Droogleever Fortuyn, Adriaan Mooy and Roelof Jongelie were dropped, all of whom were immediately arrested by the Gestapo.

CHAPTER TEN

Hermann Josef Giskes

From the German perspective, the most important person involved in Operation North Pole was Lieutenant Colonel Hermann Joseph Giskes.

Giskes was born on 28 September 1896 in the city of Krefeld, located in the North Rhine-Westphalia region of Germany. He served in the Germany Army during the First World War, enlisting on 1 October 1914 as a volunteer with Field Artillery Regiment 31, before transferring to the 2nd Bavarian Ski Battalion in December of the same year. It was whilst serving with this battalion in 1915 that he took part in campaigns in the Carpathians, South Tyrol and Serbia. In 1916 he saw action at Reims and the Battle of Verdun, during which he was severely wounded in mid-July. His actions saw him awarded the Militaerverdienstorden 3rd Class with swords and the Iron Cross 2nd Class.

In March 1917 he was promoted to the rank of Reserve Lieutenant and because he was deemed still unfit for front line service, he was utilised as an instructor with the Gebirgsjäger Battalion at Immenstadt im Allgäu.

He returned to the Western Front in April 1918 and served with the 471st Infantry Regiment as the company commander of No. 10 Company. He was captured during heavy fighting at Vaude Tres Suippe, north of Reims, on 12 October, despite some strenuous German resistance. He then became a prisoner of war at a camp for officers at Chateauroux, where he remained until his release in

1920 before returning home to Krefeld, where he began working at his father's tobacco company.

If it had not been for Operation North Pole, Giskes would more than likely have just been another faceless name who took part in the Second World War. In his book, *London Calling North Pole*, published in 1953, there is very little about his early life. The first chapter is entitled 'Summer 1941', although there is a Publisher's Note that proceeds this, which contains a miniscule amount of information about him.

Between 1936 and 1938, he completed his compulsory military service as a reserve officer, initially as a Lieutenant with the 39th Infantry Regiment in Wesel and later as a Captain with the 77th Infantry Regiment in Cologne.

In August 1938 Giskes bumped into fellow Army officer and old skiing acquaintance, Captain Feldmann, who had become a regular officer in the German Army in 1935. Feldmann suggested he should re-join the Army as he was in charge of a section of the Abwehr in Hamburg, and that a similar section was to be formed which would require an officer at the rank of Captain. Giskes did not know much about the Abwehr, or what it did, so he told Feldmann that he would think it over and in September 1938 he applied for reinstatement in the German Army. This was more for financial reasons than anything else, however, as his business had started to suffer because of the difficult economic conditions in the tobacco trade at the time, partly because of import restrictions, but also because of friction between Giskes and the local Nazi Party over his refusal to join on both religious and political grounds.

Having finally taken the advice of his friend Feldmann, Giskes began working for the Abwehr before the outbreak of the Second World War, his application being approved in November 1938, initially for a six-month probationary period, and his first day at work beginning 1 January 1939 in Hamburg.

Following the occupation of France in May 1940, he began specialising in German military counterintelligence in Paris, where he had some success in solving a series of sensational espionage cases, including one that involved officials of the American Embassy in Paris and former French General Staff officers.

Sometime in October 1940, a few British stragglers of the British Expeditionary Force (BEF) were arrested in Paris. Investigations showed they had been helped by members of the French Red Cross as well as certain individuals in the city's US Embassy. A young Russian man who was working for the Abwehr was sent to the Embassy to ask for help escaping to England. Having told his story, the young man was put in touch with a Mrs Deegan, an American employee of the Embassy, and two secretaries, Hunt and Cross. The young man ended up visited the Embassy on a number of occasions after his initial visit, which proved extremely helpful for Giskes. One of the pieces of information he passed on was the description of an English employee of the Embassy, who rarely left the building. At about the same time, another section of the Abwehr had received information that a man by the name of Sutton, who also worked at the US Embassy in Paris, was acting as a 'post box' for a spy network and that messages of an espionage nature were being sent by wireless transmission from the Embassy.

Surveillance was kept by the Geheime Feldpolizei (GFP), a military police force made up of German career police officers, who in a short period of time were able to arrest Sutton on one of the rare occasions when he ventured outside the Embassy.

By December 1940, Giskes and his office had managed to gain sufficient evidence against Mrs Deegan to arrest her for helping Allied escapees. Giskes interviewed her on two separate occasions and because of the evidence he had against her, she had no alternative but to make and sign a confession, which also implicated the secretaries Hunt and Cross.

Mrs Deegan was eventually released and initially continued to work at the US Embassy, but only until the German Foreign Office made representations to the US Government to remove her. Deegan, Hunt and Cross were all subsequently recalled to America.

It was in the autumn of 1941 when Giskes found himself working in The Hague. By 1943 he was the Chief of Military Counter-Espionage in the Netherlands, northern France and Belgium.

Soon after he had taken up residence in his new office, conveniently situated in a small, well-furnished house in the Hoogeweg in

Scheveningen, Giskes held a meeting requiring the attendance of officers from local army units as well as the Abwehr. Giskes began the meeting with the following:

> And now, gentleman, to go on to what I have to say to you. In the past few days you have individually given me a fairly clear picture of affairs. I will sum up my impressions as follows.
>
> Enemy. No active individuals or organisations are at present known with certainty to be engaged in secret service espionage or sabotage in Holland. There are, however, a few indications of such activity. The proof that forces exist in this country which are in contact with London lies in the recent unfortunate case of the Security Police on Sneeker Meer, where the party lying in wait for an enemy seaplane engaged in running agents was shot up by the aircraft itself. London must already be aware of SIPO's activities, and the enemy now holds the initiative.

Later the same day, Giskes had another meeting, this time with two unnamed officers, one of whom he referred to as Oberleutnant O, a man he knew from his time working in Paris. Both men were unit leaders within the interception and deciphering team. Some weeks before the meeting, Giskes had been informed that interception stations in Norway, Poland and southern France had reported that they had picked up short wave radio links between the Netherlands and England. The exact Dutch location had not yet been identified, but the type of radio transmissions indicated it was likely to be from agent-led type of network. The times of the communications were irregular, short in length, direct and to the point, with prompt answers all telling a story connected to agents. The radio bearings indicated that there were two transmitters operating within a triangle from Utrecht, Zeist and Amersfoort, with transmissions being sent, on average, about five times a week. The message transmission times lasted between six to nine minutes, with fourteen signals having been intercepted and accurately recorded, thus making it possible to decipher them if the required security key could be obtained.

Giskes had also been informed that a second transmitter had begun operating in the area between Delt, Gouda and Nordwijk, using the call sign TBO.

It appears that prior to Giskes' arrival, the interception of Allied radio transmissions and the desire to trace potential enemy agents operating throughout the Netherlands did not have a high level of importance.

In September 1941, Giskes travelled to Paris by car in an effort to obtain the transfer of two officers, Arno and Oswald, who had worked under him during his time in the French capital, and who he now wanted working with him in the Netherlands. Whilst in Paris he stayed in the exclusive Avenue Gabriel, which was also home to the Elysée Palace.

Having returned to his accommodation after eating his evening meal at the nearby Hotel Lutétia, he received a phone call.

Giskes picked up the receiver.

'Duty officer Lutétia speaking. Is that Dr Gerhards?' (an alias Giskes used for security reasons.)

'Speaking.'

'There is an urgent top-secret signal for you from The Hague. Will you please collect it personally?'

'Thank you. I'll come at once.'

Less than twenty minutes later, Giskes arrived at the Hotel Lutétia to collect the urgent message waiting for him. He took a corner seat in the hotel reception area, sat down, and opened the enveloped marked for his attention.

'UBX seized at 0800 today. Operator and assistant captured. Codes and extensive espionage material secured intact. When will you be back? Wurr. Oberleutnant.'

Of the two men referred to, only one of them, Johannes Zomer, was an agent, the other was the owner of the property from where the transmissions had taken place. The codes which were recovered had actually been found in the possession of the agent, Johannes Zomer, who had been dropped on 13 June 1941 by a Motor Torpedo Boat at Vledder, on the Dutch coast. He had been dropped along with fellow agent, Wiecher Bote Schrage, with both men working jointly for British MI6 and the Dutch Central Intelligence Service.

Giskes quickly realised this was a major breakthrough in the fight against Allied attempts at conducting acts of espionage throughout the occupied Netherlands.

Such was the agents' efforts to complete the sending of their message that they were still transmitting when members of the German Security Police burst in. Lieutenant Wurr, who took part in the raid, was the one who had discovered the SOE agent, along with the owner of the house, on the ground floor of a summer house in the rear garden of the property. The two men had been taken so totally by surprise that they had not reacted in time to destroy any of their equipment.

A fundamental aspect of German military counterintelligence was what they referred to as 'playing back', which in essence meant continuing to work a captured wireless set in order to hide the fact that the operative to whom it belonged had, in fact, been captured. If done correctly the link would be kept open, with the British still believing the messages being sent by the set were coming from its agent, which then meant that in return, London might just send invaluable information that would be of use to the Germans.

Because of the poor working relationship between Giskes' section and the local *Sicherheitspolizei*, or SiPO, Himmler's Security Police, it was not possible to consider utilising the 'playing back' scheme, as the SiPO had kept Johannes Zomer under their control for more than two days, during which time he would have been scheduled to have sent at least two messages back to his handlers in London. As this was not done, the worst would have been assumed and any subsequent communication from him would have been ignored.

Zomer was subsequently charged with conducting espionage for an enemy nation and put before a German military court. Found guilty, he was executed by firing squad on 11 May 1942.

The second chapter of Giskes' book provides an extremely interesting insight into how the German Abwehr used what were known as 'V-men'. Throughout the Netherlands during the Second World War, the Gestapo employed these Dutch men, who were prepared to work for them by infiltrating different organisations, including political groups and the Dutch resistance.

In November 1941 Giskes' section in The Hague was contacted by a man by the name of Ridderhoff who claimed to know of English agents located in the city, and for a sum of money he would be more than happy to pass on the information he had. One of Giskes' men, known only as 'Willy', met with Ridderhoff on 27 November 1941. His account of that meeting included the following:

> Personal for head of IIIF. Today at 1300 hours second meeting with Ridderhoff, American Hotel, Amsterdam. R states he is contact with Dutch reserve officer who works for two British agents operating probably in The Hague. R. needs money. Also asks for protection under against the German currency authorities, who have had him in custody charged with diamond smuggling. Request interview with Chief 1700 hours 28th November at headquarters. Willy.

The two agents referred to could well have been Huub Lauwers and Thijs Taconis, who had been dropped into the Netherlands on 6 November 1941 and remained at large until March 1942.

Ridderhoff was given the code name of 'George' and the reference number 'F2087'. What is known about Ridderhoff is from a description of him by Willy that he gave to Giskes when the latter asked about him.

'He lives in Baarn, Chief, and is allegedly in business. When in drink he speaks a mixture of Spanish, English and Dutch. He is a large, fat, bloated sort of fellow, lame in the left leg, a type you can pick out of a hundred.'

'Good,' Giskes replied. 'Get a photo, under the pretext of getting him a false pass. You are quite clear, I hope, that we are only concerned in uncovering the agents and their collaborators at The Hague? Keep George strictly on the rails. No new ideas and no side-tracking until that is cleared up. Got it?'

'*Jawohl*, Chief!' replied Willy, who could not help but feel a little excited about the job he had been given. Ridderhoff quickly became a full-time commitment for Willy, and the more time and effort he put in, the more Ridderfoff opened up to him and trusted him. Willy's next report included information that the two British Agents possessed a radio transmitter. Over the following weeks, Willy and Ridderoff's meetings became more frequent. Then, on

10 December 1941, Willy sent another report to Giskes: 'Source F2087. Agent Two at The Hague is looking out for suitable sites for dropping weapons and sabotage material by parachute. The timing will be arranged with London and a reception committee detailed by him. A widespread organisation is being planned, which will be systematically armed and trained.'

Despite Willy's belief that this was the start of something big, Giskes was not as easily convinced, and even wrote in the margin of the report, 'Go to the North Pole with your stories. There is no radio communication between Holland and England. F2087 has three days in which to clear up this contradiction in terms!'

Giskes, who having fully digested the report from Willy, found himself in somewhat of a bad mood, and so contacted one of his subordinate officers, Lieutenant Heinrichs, wanting to know why the German intercept stations under his command had not identified the particular radio transmissions which Willy had mentioned in his report. Heinrichs assured him that his men were working around the clock and had not come across any such radio traffic, calming Giskes down in the process.

After a brief conversation with his deputy, Wurr, he even considered the possibility that the reason why Heinrichs' men were not picking up any traffic between Holland and London was because different radio frequencies, on a different type of wireless set, were being used by the British. Wurr told Giskes that he had heard from Berlin that 'great progress had been made in the design of VHF sets for agents' use'.

Willy's next report brought a smile to Giskes' face:

F2087 had been in close contact with Reserve Captain v.d Berg at The Hague since 12 December. Berg had accepted F2807's offer to take care of the transfer of certain material which will be delivered from England. Drops are not expected for the time being as the radio link with England is not in operation. The set appears to be defective, and efforts are being made to repair it.

Ridderhoff's credibility sky-rocketed when he provided information that three men were to be picked up by a British Motor Torpedo

Boat (MTB) from the beach at Scheveningen. No date was provided, but the pickup would take place between 21:00 and 01:00 on the same night that a particular tune was played over Radio Orange, a BBC channel from the UK.

In late January 1942, the tune that Giskes had been waiting for was played over Radio Orange, and three men were discovered and arrested later that evening at roughly the same location indicated as the pick-up point. No MTB had been discovered, and the three men came up with a story that they had been to a party and were simply relieving themselves. This was a delicate situation for Giskes because the last thing he wanted to do was to raise any suspicions that might ultimately be connected to Ridderhoff.

It is clear reading through the pages of Giskes' book that the start of Operation North Pole came about as a result of hard work by the men of his section and their connection with Reserve Captain van der Berg who worked in the Hague, and Ridderhoff, a Dutchman who had been arrested for diamond smuggling. It would appear that both men were, for their own reasons, prepared to provide Giskes' men with useful information. When talking about 'early January 1942', Giskes says in his book, 'From v.d Berg, learnt that a plan to take three men by MTB from the coast of Scheveningen to England was in course of preparation.' In fact, Giskes does not make any mention of being helped by a British spy who worked at the very heart of British military intelligence, and by the time he wrote his book, he would have had no reason to hide the name of any such person, should one have ever existed.

Another interesting aspect of the book is it appears he had requested all captured agents should be kept together at the old seminary at Haaren so that they were available for questioning at very short notice. There is, however, nothing about Giskes having promised to keep the captured agents alive. One interpretation could be that the reason why the SOE/MI6 agents were moved from Haaren in April 1944 was because of the escape from that location of three of the agents held there. This was not a decision that he had any control over.

Giskes makes the following comment about this situation in his book:

The whereabouts and the fate of the *Nordpol* agents gave me increasing anxiety after our retreat from Holland in September 1944, my attempts to retain some control over the fate of these men after the end of *Nordpol* having been brought to nothing by their transfer to Assen. The sharp deterioration of our relations with the head of the Sicherheitspolizei in Holland had caused us to lose all influence over their subsequent treatment.

As an agent caught working for Britain and or her allies, dressed in either civilian clothes or German military uniform was liable to be shot by firing squad under rules of the Geneva convention, it is unclear as to why Giskes would have any real concern for the lives of those agents captured as part of Operation North Pole. Maybe it was genuine rhetoric on his part. Maybe spouting such a narrative made him feel better about himself, or he said it because he believed it would help distance himself from the obvious dangers of being connected to the murderous elements of his Nazi paymasters.

In October 1944 Giskes and his men moved to Brussels, their work in the Netherlands having come to an end. Their new 'home' was a large building in the capital's Place de l'Industrie. It was a move which in some respects seemed at odds with the course of the war, as life for German soldiers in Belgium was a lot more dangerous than it was for those stationed in the Netherlands. Despite a number of Abwehr officers having been murdered in the Belgian capital, it did not prevent Giskes and the Abwehr from quietly and effectively carrying on their work.

Lieutenant Colonel Hermann Giskes was captured wearing civilian clothes whilst hiding in buildings at Wiehl, in North Rhine-Westphalia, which had been in use as the training school for German agents of FAK 307. After being provisionally interrogated in the field, he was brought to England on 24 May 1945 for a more detailed interrogation, and to be detained at what was known as Camp 020 at Latchmere House in southwest London. There he was interviewed by a number of military intelligence officers, including Robert Maxwell, who after the war worked in publishing before becoming a Member of Parliament for Buckingham and then returning to publishing to become the owner of Mirror Group Newspapers.

A file is held on Giskes at The National Archives in London under the reference KV 2/963. It contains numerous references about different agencies wanting sight of a copy of his post-war interview at Camp 020, but there is no actual copy of the interview contained within the file, which concludes with the following comments: 'Preliminary investigation indicates that GISKES is providing a mass of useful accurate information. He gives every appearance of being fully co-operative; it is apparent that he is a bitter enemy of the Gestapo and did all he could not only to save captured Allied agents from ill-treatment, but also to try and have their lives spared.'

Unfortunately, there is no attached account of how Giskes had tried to prevent the ill-treatment and/or death of captured British Agents.

A second file on Giskes exists with a reference number of KV 2/961. In it, Giskes provides an interesting explanation as to how the greeting parties, who had to be in place on the ground to meet arriving SOE agents, were contacted. This was done by phone by one of his officers, usually Wurr, and would be worded along the following lines: 'We would like to invite you to a little party this evening at Wochenendhaus. We shall have some guests and would be delighted if you could come along. A couple of "Damen" are also coming. Bring a couple of partners for them so they don't become bored.'

In such a message the word 'Damen' was used to indicate the arrival of agents.

One of the claims in this file is extremely interesting. Shortly after Huub Lauwers' arrest, who is referred to throughout by his code name of 'Ebenezer', one of Giskes' team, an officer by the name of Kup, paid him a visit and afterwards reported back to Giskes that he was prepared to work for the Germans. Giskes maintains that no physical force was used against him in an effort to make him assist the Germans. Giskes also visited Lauwers in prison and claims that he guaranteed him his life, as well as the lives of any subsequent Allied agent who followed him. On agreeing to work for the Germans, Lauwers told Giskes that before leaving on his mission, he had been assured by an officer named Colonel Blunt that in the event of his capture, he was free to accept any proposal to work for the Germans, in an effort to save his life, because at the most it would take the British less than three weeks to determine if he was transmitting his messages under German control.

Giskes further claimed that Albert Arnoldus Baatsen, code named 'Watercress', voluntarily offered to work for the Germans after he landed in the Netherlands on 28 March 1942, and was arrested soon after. Giskes claimed he spied on his fellow prisoners at the old seminary at Haaren for the SD. Apparently, Gozewijn Hendrik Gerard Ras, code named 'Lettuce', Hendrik Johan Jordaan, code named 'Trumpet', and Leonardus Andringa, code named 'Turnip', were his targets.

The interrogation of these three men produced a full and comprehensive account about the dropping operation on 28 March 1942, including the name of the agent who had been killed on landing. What was even more concerning is Giskes' claim that the three men also provided the numbers of Dutch SOE agents who had completed their training, and who could therefore be expected to arrive in the Netherlands soon. They also produced descriptions of the agents, any aliases, and what their area of expertise was.

In one statement made by Giskes, his words could be interpreted in such a way as to make it appear that he too was a victim. He talks about 'Nordpol' coming to an end, along with the escapes by SOE agents who were held at Haaren.

This led to a severe conflict with a corresponding sharp exchange of letters between C-in-C Holland and the Hoehere S.S and Polizeifuehrer. This culminated in the suggestion that the Abwehr officer responsible for the affair, namely myself, was to blame for the fact that the matter had become blown to the enemy, owing to the fact that up to the present, he has obstructed sentence being passed on the prisoners.

The continuation of my work in Holland was then, for all practical purposes, at an end and I came to the conclusion that the S.D. intended to have me locked up and disposed of in some manner.

The file concludes with the following observations and comments about Giskes by an unnamed source working at Camp 020:

> Giskes is a German officer and was a very astute member of the Abwehr. He is intelligent and realises that the fact he was taken in plain clothes, trying to avoid capture, has prejudiced his position considerably; this circumstance has probably rendered him more co-operative than he might otherwise have been. He also is aware that information that he gives can be checked, with the result that he has been found to be a fruitful and accurate source.
>
> He has been directly responsible for the arrest of a number of S.O.E. agents in Holland, but interrogation of one of these agents now in the UK, bears out Giskes' contention that he did his utmost to protect them from the ministrations of the SiPO.
>
> Giskes, both in Holland and Belgium, was always playing for higher stakes than the suppression and arrest of espionage and Resistance Groups; his aims were to effect contact with Allied Intelligence Services in order to discover their plans and to carry out deception, in these two aims he was remarkably successful.
>
> Giskes is now a middle-aged man with no prospects in a chaotic Germany; it is thought unlikely that he has, or knows of, any long-term plans for the rehabilitation of the Abwehr, but he might, if released, gravitate towards such a movement if it existed now, or in the future. Giskes, although strongly anti-Nazi at whose hands he has to a certain extent suffered, is before everything a German officer, and as such, could be a danger in the future if he were to come under the influence of brother officers working for the resurrection of a pre-Nazi Germany.

With the SOE having been disbanded at the end of the Second World War, and with most of the files outlining the work carried out by Dutch agents deployed to the Netherlands having been inexplicably destroyed, certain high-ranking military officers, and maybe even some senior politicians, had no doubt hoped that whatever had gone on was simply going to go away and disappear as if it had never happened. This perhaps would have been true, if it had not been for the publication of Giskes' book.

It would be fair to say that the book's publication opened a massive can of worms and left the British government and military officials having to suddenly answer some extremely awkward questions.

One of the first things that catches the eye when looking at the book's contents page is that it contains an epilogue by Huub Lauwers, one of the actual SOE spies who was captured as part of operation North Pole.

Lauwers begins his epilogue by saying that, 'It may cause surprise to find in an account by the former Chief of German Military Counterintelligence of his war time activities, an epilogue from the hand of one of his defeated adversaries. I must therefore explain how this has come about.'

He then goes on to explain that everything published up to that point in time had come from German controlled documents and reports, some of which did not always reflect well on himself and his fellow SOE agents who had been caught up in Operation North Pole. There were even comments made at an official level suggesting that both he and his colleague, Taconis, were traitors. By adding an epilogue, Lauwers felt that it was his opportunity to put right some of the wrongs that had been made about what had really taken place. Having said that, it is still rather strange to have a book written by Hermann Giskes containing an epilogue by Lauwers.

In the immediate aftermath of the Second World War there was a thirst for information about events which had taken place, especially in books written by those involved in the events themselves. Many stories could not be told because the subject matter was still deemed to be 'Top Secret', or witnesses were unavailable to contribute to the book to provide a balanced account of the story.

In Giskes' case he had been an officer in the German Army and had not been a Nazi or a member of the SS; he had simply done his job to the best of his ability, in a fair and balanced way, which meant that a German writing a book about matters that ultimately led to the deaths of Dutch agents whilst working for the British SOE were more 'palatable' to the general public. By the early 1950s, people had come to realise what they were being told via the government and other official channels was not necessarily the full story or contained the complete truth for that matter. For Giskes, it was an opportunity to make some much needed money in an uncertain post war world.

After finally being released by the British, Giskes went on to work for US intelligence services throughout Europe. He died on 27 August 1977 in Krefeld, aged 80.

CHAPTER ELEVEN

Discussions in Parliament about Operation North Pole

What happened in the eighteen months of Operation North Pole gripped people's imaginations for years after the events, both politicians and civilians alike. Between January 1953 and May 1966 there were a number of debates which took place in Parliament that were directly connected to Operation North Pole, and which were recorded in Hansard. What follows are excerpts from these official parliamentary transcripts.

On 28 January 1953, a brief debate took place under the heading 'British Secret Service (Mr H.M.G. Lauwers)'. Mr Arthur Lewis, the Labour MP for the constituency of Westham North, asked the Conservative MP for Warwick and Leamington, who also held the post of Secretary of State for Foreign Affairs, Mr Anthony Eden, what rank and position Lauwers held with his department during 1942-43; what duties were allotted to him; and what position he now held.

Mr Eden replied:

Mr Lauwers was recruited as a wireless transmitter operator by the Joint British-Netherlands section of the Special Operations Executive, a now defunct organisation, which, during its lifetime was under the direction of the Minister of Economic Warfare. In late 1941 he was parachuted into

Holland and captured by the Germans. I understand that Mr Lauwers is a Netherlands national, and I am unaware of the position he now holds.

Mr Lewis continued by asking Mr Eden why British official witnesses were refused permission to give evidence before a parliamentary Commission held at The Hague and presided over by the present Dutch Minister of Justice, to inquire into alleged neglect on the part of the British Secret Service.

Mr Eden stated that:

His late Majesty's government welcomed the Netherlands official inquiry and while it is true that no British official witnesses attended the hearings of the Netherlands Parliamentary Commission at The Hague, representatives of the Commission were invited to London, where arrangements were made for them to meet and question British officials concerned.

Mr Lewis then continued the debate by asking Mr Eden if he was aware that during 1942-43, fifty-four British agents fell into German hands, forty-seven of whom were subsequently executed at Mauthausen, through the deception perpetrated on the British Secret Service by Lieutenant H.M.G. Lauwers, a British Secret Service agent; and what action was taken on this matter.

Mr Eden responded by saying:

The figures given by the hon. Member are, so far as I am aware, substantially correct, though I cannot accept the implication of the responsibility of Mr Lauwers. Appropriate action was taken immediately on discovery of the deception perpetrated by the Germans.

I understand that the matter was the subject of a full inquiry at the time. After the war further inquiries were conducted by the British and Netherlands authorities.

Mr Eden's final reply was interesting as it mentions that appropriate action was taken immediately once the German deception had been discovered. What he failed to say, however, was that by the time of the discovery, some eighteen months had passed and more than fifty agents had been captured by the German authorities.

He provided no details of when the full inquiry he mentioned took place, or the names of those who took part in it. Somewhat surprisingly, Mr Lewis did not challenge him on either point.

On 30 January 1953, a brief debate took place under the heading of 'British Secret Service (Allegations)'. In it, Mr Lewis asked the Secretary of State for Foreign Affairs, Mr Anthony Nutting, the Conservative MP for Melton, whether he would move to appoint a Select Committee to inquire into all matters pertaining to allegations of neglect made against the British Secret Service and Foreign Office by Lieutenant Colonel H.J. Giskes in his book, *London Calling North Pole,* a copy of which had been sent to him.

Mr Nutting replied, 'No. These matters were fully and adequately investigated both at the time of their occurrence and afterwards.'

Although an extremely brief exchange between the two men, it can only be assumed that Mr Lewis was happy with the reply as he did not push the matter any further. It is also abundantly clear that the only reason such a topic had found itself being discussed in Parliament was because of the publication of Giskes' book.

A continuation of the debate between the two men continued the following week, on Wednesday, 4 February, still under the heading of 'British Secret Service (Allegations)'.

Mr Lewis asked the Secretary of State for Foreign Affairs if he would publish the information submitted to the representatives of the Netherlands Parliamentary Commission at The Hague held in 1948-50, on the occasion of their visit to London to question the British officials concerned in the allegations against the British Secret Service.

Mr Nutting replied that a summary of the information given to the Commission was published in the Commission's report in 1950.

Mr Lewis then asked the following question:

Is the Minister aware of the fact that the Foreign Office issued a statement to the effect that they could not hold an inquiry at the time because the officers and men concerned were not available, and that is appreciated and understood and that subsequently, when an inquiry was asked for, the Foreign Office said that they had destroyed all the documents and papers which would verify the Netherlands Government's claim that there had been serious neglect on the part of the British Secret Service? Does the Joint Under-Secretary not think that this matter warrants a further and proper inquiry?

Mr Nutting replied that 'The hon. Member has already been told in answer to other questions, that this matter was at no stage and at no time a responsibility of the Foreign Office. The Minister responsible for the Special Operations Executive during the war was the Minister of Economic Warfare.'

Mr Lewis then pointed out that it was the Foreign Office that wound up this organisation, destroyed very important secret documents, and that now the German officer in charge of the German counterespionage service had evidence to prove there was near treachery on the part of this particular officer. He then asked whether Mr Nutting thought this needed thorough investigation?

Mr Nutting, who by now was no doubt feeling somewhat under pressure due to Mr Lewis' questions, replied that there was no treachery on the part of Mr Lauwers.

Continuing with his questions, Mr Lewis then asked Mr Nutting if he would provide the reasons for the arrest in 1944 of Pieter Dourlein and Johan Ubbink, the two British agents employed by the joint British/Netherlands section of the Special Operations Executive following their escape from a German prison and return to England. How long and for what reasons were these men kept under arrest; what charges were made against them when their trial took place; and what was the result?

Mr Nutting replied that Dourlein and Ubbink were detained for security reasons under the 1837 Aliens Order from 27 May to 20 June, and that as no charge was made against them, the latter part of the question was irrelevant.

Mr Lewis then asked whether the minister was aware that these two men were agents in the very department who had nearly been condemned to death because of neglect on the part of the British

Secret Service, and that when they came back to protest and produce their evidence, they were not allowed to submit it, were put under arrest with no charges and kept there. He questioned whether it was not time that investigations were made into the allegations that had been made, and the men given an opportunity of coming forward. He also pointed out that the two men had been awarded the equivalent of the British VC by the Netherlands government, on whose behalf they worked.

In response, Mr Nutting said the men's detention was ordered as part of the exceptional, but necessary, security precautions and were taken during the period of the invasion of Europe. The fact they were detained was no reflection upon the men themselves, but merely a security precaution designed to ensure that the story of their escape was a genuine one.

The debate threw up a couple of extremely interesting points, which despite the conversation between the two men, were not fully clarified. Mr Lewis highlighted the point that important documents concerning the case had been destroyed, but when Mr Nutting failed to even address this, Mr Lews did not press him on the matter at all, meaning the reason why these documents were destroyed, by whom, under whose instruction and when, was never established.

The other point worth examining is Mr Nutting's reply relating to the arrest of Pieter Dourlein and Johan Ubbink, who he said were detained for security reasons under the 1837 Aliens Order. In essence this meant arresting people who were caught entering the country without a passport. Although Mr Lewis may have found the men's arrest as possibly unnecessary, but with the nation at war, and two men turning up on English soil, both with foreign sounding accents and no passports or any other form of conclusive identification, their arrest would have surely been an obvious and necessary step to take.

Later the same day, Mr Lewis asked a further question of Mr Nutting connected to Operation North Pole, although it is recorded in Hansard as 'Captured British Agents, Mauthausen (Inquiry)'. This time, Mr Lewis asked Mr Nutting if he would publish the report of the full inquiry held at the time, and the further inquiries after the war by the British authorities into the capture and death of forty-seven British agents during 1942-43 at Mauthausen.

Mr Nutting informed him that a summary of the information from the inquiries was communicated to the Netherlands Parliamentary Commission and published as an annex to its report in 1950.

Mr Lewis' question was slightly incorrect in that the captured Dutch SOE agents from Operation North Pole did not arrive at Mauthausen concentration camp until sometime in September 1944, and the subsequent murder of forty-seven of those agents took place sometime after that date.

On 5 February 1953, under the same heading of 'British Secret Service (Allegations)', Mr Lewis once again took the opportunity to press Mr Nutting on the matter of Operation North Pole, asking the Secretary of State whether he would agree to meet a deputation consisting of the hon. Member for West Ham, North, representatives of the Dutch underground services, and Mr P. Kimber, publisher of Hermann Giskes' book, in which allegations of neglect and mistakes on the part of Special Operations Executive, and the British Secret Service during the Second World War were itemised, to enable them to submit further evidence in connection will these matters and to discuss them with him.

Mr Nutting would not be swayed on the matter and replied accordingly, which brought the parliamentary exchange between the two men to an abrupt end, as Mr Lewis did not see fit to continue the matter any further.

Just four days later, on Monday, 9 February, and under the same heading, Mr Lewis asked yet another question in Parliament, this time in relation to the inquiry which had previously taken place and which had looked into allegations made about the actions of the British Secret Service as part of Operation North Pole.

Mr Lewis asked the Secretary of State what type of inquiry was held both at the time and subsequently into allegations of neglect on the part of the British Secret Service in respect of the case outlined in Giskes' book, whether Huub Lauwers, Pieter Dourlein, Johan Ubbink and Giskes gave oral or written evidence at either of these inquiries, and the terms of reference of these inquiries.

This time, Mr Lewis' question was answered by the Minister of State for Foreign Affairs, Mr Selwyn Lloyd, who declared he had nothing further to add to what had already been said.

Unshaken, Mr Lewis wondered how there could have been a proper inquiry when the vital witnesses had not given any evidence, either orally or in writing? In view of the fact that the whole of the evidence was destroyed within two years of the end of the war, he asked whether a thorough inquiry would be made into the matter, like the Netherlands Parliamentary Commission of Inquiry in Holland.

Mr Lloyd's response was that if Mr Lewis had any new substantial evidence to bring forward, then the Foreign Secretary would be pleased to receive it. He also refused to answer a further question about whether the officers directly connected with the incident would give evidence.

On Wednesday, 11 February 1953, and under the heading of 'British Secret Service (Allegations)', a brief debate once again took place between Mr Lewis and Anthony Nutting.

Mr Lewis asked the Secretary of State how many of the forty-seven British agents who were executed by the Germans at Mauthausen during 1942-43 were of British nationality, and what were their names and ranks.

In response Mr Nutting replied that none of the agents who had been murdered at Mauthausen were British, meaning that the second part of his question was not relevant.

Mr Lewis' response was to enquire if the three surviving agents had provided any evidence at the so-called Foreign Office inquiry into the murders of the murdered agents, which the Foreign Office had already admitted was due to neglect by the SOE.

Mr Nutting stated that he could not say who had given evidence at the inquiry, and that Mr Lewis should put forward that question separately if he wished it addressed.

Later the same day another Parliamentary debate took place between Mr Lewis and Mr Nutting, this time under the heading of 'British Secret Service (War Time Activities)'. Mr Lewis asked Mr Nutting on what date or dates, the papers, documents, secret wireless messages to and from British agents employed by SOE were destroyed; how many of these papers and documents in total were destroyed; and what was the reason for the hurried destruction of these documents in view of the request of the Netherlands Government to have them for their Parliamentary Commission of

Inquiry into alleged neglect on the part of the officials connected with that department?

Mr Nutting informed Mr Lewis that when the SOE had been wound up at the end of the war, only those documents considered necessary for the maintenance of official records were destroyed, explaining that he could not say with any degree of accuracy how many such documents were destroyed or when.

Undeterred, Mr Lewis continued by asking Mr Nutting if he was aware of similar incidents involving twenty-five SOE agents who had been dropped into Belgium during the war into German hands? Did he know what had happened to these men; what were their names and rank; and what inquiry was held into the cause of this mistake?

Mr Nutting responded by explaining that during the war a number of SOE agents were parachuted into Belgium, some of whom were caught whilst others were not. He further explained that some of those captured were executed by the Germans, but he was not prepared to disclose their names or ranks. Mr Nutting finished by explaining that a comprehensive inquiry was carried out and any appropriate action had been taken.

Mr Lewis continued bombarding Mr Nutting with questions about SOE wartime operations, in particular asking if the three SOE agents who were not executed by the Germans had provided any information at an inquiry held by the Foreign Office into the matter?

Mr Nutting's reply seemed somewhat at odds with what he was saying, 'I cannot say offhand exactly who gave evidence at the inquiry that was held at the time and after the war. Perhaps the hon. Gentleman will put down that question.' Surely he would have had such information ready to hand? It certainly supports the theory of there having been some kind of official government cover up.

Two days later, on Friday, 13 February, the two men crossed swords once again on the subject of the British Secret Service, with Mr Lewis asked Mr Nutting if he would give a list of all positions and appointments held in the Government services by Mr Seymour, Colonel Cordeaux and Colonel Rabagliatti of the Intelligence Service and the date of such appointments. Mr Nutting's reply was certainly succinct: 'No.'

Undeterred by the response Mr Lewis continued and asked Mr Nutting if he would publish the report of the conversations which took place between Colonel Cordeaux and Colonel Rabagliatti and representatives of the Netherlands Parliamentary Commission of Inquiry between 3 and 10 October 1949. He received the same reply: 'No.'

In this instance, Colonel Cordeaux is, I believe, a reference to Lieutenant Colonel John Kyme Cordeaux, who is shown as having served with the Royal Marines during the Second World War. He was made a CBE in 1946. Meanwhile, Colonel Cuthbert Rabagliati, MC, AFC was an officer in the British Army who served as the head of the Dutch Section of the Secret Intelligence Service.

Just three days later, on Monday, 16 February, Mr Lewis took part in yet another debate connected to Operation North Pole under the heading of 'British Secret Service (War Time Activities)'. This time he found himself up against Mr Anthony Eden, the Secretary of State for Foreign Affairs.

Mr Lewis asked Mr Eden what position Mr Guy Burgess had held in the Ministry of Economic Warfare, Special Operations Executive, during the war; what was the nature of his duties; and to what extent, if any, he had any connection with any of the agents who were subsequently executed by the Germans at Mauthausen.

Mr Eden's response to all the questions was short and to the point: 'None, Sir.'

Mr Lewis thanked Mr Eden for his reply before trying to illicit from him whether he knew if Guy Burgess had any connection with the SOE, as contacts he had with the Dutch underground movement stated was the case.

Mr Eden responded by informing Mr Lewis that as far as he knew, Burgess had begun working for the BBC sometime in 1941, and therefore could not have been involved in events in the Netherlands during 1942-43.

Although Eden's reply was correct, he conveniently forgot to mention Section D of the SOE, which was established by MI6 in March 1938 as a secret organisation charged with investigating how enemies might be attacked other than through military operations. It was Burgess' job to act as Section D's representative on the Joint

Broadcasting Committee (JBC), a body which had been set up by the Foreign Office to liaise with the BBC over the transmission of anti-Hitler broadcasts to Germany.

After the outbreak of the Second World War in September 1939, Burgess, along with fellow Russian spy, Kim Philby, who had been brought into Section D on his recommendation, began running a training course for future British and Allied spies and saboteurs, at Brickendonbury Manor in Hertfordshire. This appears to be somewhat of a strange decision as neither man had any real idea of what would actually be expected of an agent in the field, behind enemy lines, in occupied Europe.

Although Burgess did in fact work for the BBC in January 1941, it is believed that he also continued to carry out 'freelance' work for MI6 as well as MI5, information which Anthony Eden would have quite clearly been aware of.

The following day, Tuesday, 17 June, saw Mr Lewis ask yet another question of Mr Nutting, this time under the heading of 'Special Operations Executive'.

Mr Lewis asked if the names and ranks of the officers in charge of the Special Operations Executive during the war would be revealed, and what positions these men subsequently went on to hold. Unsurprisingly, his request was denied, being informed that it would not be in the public interest to disclose such information.

In some respects, Mr Lewis' request was rather ambiguous, as the SOE had been disbanded at the end of the war and some eight years before this debate took place, meaning there was every possibility that most, if not all, these officers would no longer be members of the armed forces.

Later the same day Mr Lewis asked yet another question of Mr Nutting, again in relation to Guy Burgess. This time it was concerning what position he had held in connection with the operations which had involved British Secret Service agents parachuting into German-held Belgium.

Mr Nutting replied: 'None.'

Although Mr Lewis did not mention how many parachute drops he was referring to, or any specific dates, for Mr Nutting to answer as he did suggests that he was fully aware of what Mr Lewis was referring to.

Mr Lewis and Mr Nutting faced each other yet again the following day. By now Mr Nutting must have been close to mental exhaustion, as there appeared to be no likelihood of any let up on the part of Mr Lewis in his quest to find out the truth behind Operation North Pole and whether or not there had been any kind of cover up by the British Government or elements within the secret service.

Once again, the heading of the brief interaction between the two men in the House of Commons was 'British Secret Service (Allegations)'.

This time Mr Lewis asked Mr Nutting for the names of those who gave evidence at the inquiries into allegations of neglect on the part of the British Secret Service in connection with the execution of the agents at Mauthausen, and how many of those agents who escaped execution were called to give evidence.

Mr Nutting informed Mr Lewis that he could not reveal the information he required as what he was asking related to a secret organisation, and it therefore would not be in the public interest to do so make such matters public.

This appeared to be a very lazy and yet convenient reply. By this time, such information would not have been useful to an enemy, as the nation was no longer at war. In relation to the public interest aspect of Nutting's answer, this also appears way off the mark, as it was a topic which would have no doubt have been of great interest to a large section of the British public.

Yet Mr Lewis was like the proverbial bull in a China shop. His doggedness on getting to the truth was unswerving in its determination and he did not have to wait too long to challenge Mr Nutting again. In fact, just two days later, on Friday, 20 February, the two men once again went toe-to-toe across the floor of the House of Commons, when the allegations in relation to the British Secret Service were once again discussed.

Mr Lewis asked Mr Nutting if he would arrange to have placed in the House of Commons Library a copy of the annex to the report of the Netherlands Parliamentary Commission of Inquiry, dated

1950, wherein allegations of neglect against Special Operations Executive and the British Secret Service were made.

Mr Nutting side stepped the question by referring him to a previous answer he had given in relation to a document referred to in a statement made by the Foreign Office to Dr Donker, Chairman of the Netherlands Parliamentary Commission of Inquiry into the conduct of clandestine operations in Holland, dated 14 December 1949.

Mr Lewis then asked if a copy of the statement made by Mr Nutting's Department to Dr Donker would be published in the parliamentary record?

Mr Nutting's response was to inform Mr Lewis that as the statement referred to was a lengthy one, he would place a copy of it in the library.

It is interesting to note that although Mr Nutting agreed to Mr Lewis' request, the latter did not actually ask for a copy of the report.

What drove Mr Lewis in his almost incessant pursuit to uncover information in relation to Operation North Pole is unclear and continues to remain unanswered. There is certainly no known explanation as to why he did not simply table all the questions he had on the topic in one session rather than spread them out as he did.

On 2 March Mr Lewis asked two questions under the heading of 'British Secret Service (Allegations)'. The first was answered by Mr Selwyn Lloyd, the Minister of State for Foreign Affairs, whilst the second was answered by Mr Nutting.

Mr Lewis asked Mr Lloyd three questions. The first was whether he had considered a letter from the hon. Member for West Ham, North, which enclosed the communication from Colonel Dr J.M. Somer, the former Commanding Officer of the Dutch Bureau Inlichtingen, which contained evidence of continuing neglect on the part of British Secret Service agents during the war; and whether he would make a statement in answer to the points contained in the Colonel's letter.

His second question concerned the 3,000 Sten guns, 300 Bren guns, 2,000 hand grenades, 75 radio transmitters and secret radar equipment which had been parachuted into the Netherlands during the war by British Secret Service agents after the Service had been informed that its agents were actually in the hands of the Germans.

His third and final question was why, and on what basis, the British Secret Service had made arrangements for van der Waals, a German Secret Service agent employed by the Gestapo, to be introduced to Mr Vorrink, the leader of the Dutch Underground Movement, as an Allied friend and British agent, and would he explain the procedure that had been adopted to inform Mr Vorrink that van der Waals was a tried and trusted friend of Great Britain.

Mr Lloyd answered the first question by telling Mr Lewis that he had been repeatedly informed that these matters had been the subject of a full investigation both during and after the war. As Mr Lewis had also been told on 18 February, it was not in the public interest to publish details of the affairs of secret organisations.

The Foreign Office statement of 14 December 1949, annexed to the Netherlands Parliamentary Commission's report, admitted that mistakes were made. It made it clear, however, that the inquiries had not revealed the slightest grounds for believing that there was treachery either on the British or on the Netherlands side, a statement endorsed by the Netherlands Parliamentary Commission. The letter from Colonel Somer, however, dated 10 February, was not received in Mr Lloyd's department until 26 February, and there had not been time for detailed examination of its contents. It did not appear, however, to contain anything new or which would justify further discussion with Dr Somer.

Mr Lewis then asked Mr Nutting if he would arrange to invite Colonel Dr J.M. Somers, the former Commanding Officer of the Dutch Secret Service, to the UK so that he may submit his evidence of neglect on the part of the British Intelligence during the last war to an independent committee of inquiry?

Mr Nutting's response was brief, informing Mr Lewis that he had nothing further to add to replies already given to him earlier in the day.

Mr Lewis had asked some very good questions, but for some reason the establishment appeared determined not to answer them with any degree of clarity. In taking such a stance, all they actually achieved was to add to the confusion and doubt over what had actually taken place, which in turn made it appear that they were not being completely honest. This simply led to even more questions, the main one being, why?

An interesting article appeared in the *Sunday Dispatch* daily newspaper on Sunday, 29 November 1953 about the state of the British Secret Service. It was not solely in relation to Operation North Pole, however, but also included other incidents where MI6 had been found to be lacking. Part of the article said the following:

In the House of Commons, Mr Arthur Lewis, Socialist MP for West Ham, has tried more than twenty times this year to obtain answers to questions about the Secret Services.

Mr Lewis wanted to know who were the men whose 'errors of judgement' led to the deaths of forty-seven Dutch patriots. It is alleged that during the war no attention was paid to a warning sent by pre-arranged code signal from the Dutch underground. As a result, Dutch agents were parachuted into Holland and forty-seven of them were captured and executed.

Mr Lewis' questions were only partially answered and his questioning in the commons was blocked on the subject.

A Netherlands Parliamentary Commission of Inquiry spoke of the tragedy as a result of 'serious blunders'. The British Foreign Office used the phrase 'errors of judgement'.

But the Foreign Office admitted that serious obstacles were put in the way of the inquiry because the bulk of the records of the British controlled organisation involved was destroyed immediately after the war when it (the SOE) was dissolved. These included the actual wireless messages to and from the Netherlands.

Criticism has also been levelled at the British Secret Services on the same matter in books written by the chief of German counterespionage in Holland, Colonel H.J. Giskes, and one of the Dutch agents who escaped, Pieter Dourlein.

Colonel Giskes in his book, "Calling North Pole," says: 'If the [British] radio organisations had observed proper security precautions, we should never have been able to introduce our own operators. But since our experience hitherto had not disclosed any special degree of watchfulness on their part, we took the risk. The carelessness of the enemy is illustrated by the fact that more than fourteen different radio links were established with London for longer or shorter periods during the Nordpol operation, and these fourteen were operated by six of our own operators.'

The part of the article which mentions the bulk of the records concerning the SOE's involvement in Operation North Pole, which included copies of the actual messages sent and received between London and the Netherlands, destroyed at the end of the war, could be taken as a strong indicator that British authorities did in fact try to cover up something connected to the operation.

What is not clear is whether this was in relation to covering up British incompetence in the affair, the fact that Britain knew the German operators were the ones sending messages but continued with the charade so as not to let the Germans know that they knew, or to cover up the fact that there was a German spy secreted within the British Secret Service, which if that was the case, would have been highly embarrassing, as well as damaging for the organisation.

Nearly three years passed before there was any further mention of the SOE or the agency's involvement in Operation North Pole in either the House of Commons or Parliament, but on 22 February 1956, Dame Irene Ward, the Conservative MP for Tynemouth asked why files and documents concerning the SOE and their wartime actions across Europe had been made available by some of these occupied nations to British writers and historians, but the same information was not made available by the relevant authorities in Britain.

She also wanted to ascertain why SOE files on agents operating behind enemy lines in the course of their duties, and who did not return after the war, had not been made available to British historians, so that they in turn were able to provide accounts of their actions for the consumption by the general public. She pointed out that such files being made available would also provide an explanation to the families of those same agents as to what had happened to their loved ones.

In response, Lord John Hope, the Joint Under Secretary of State for Foreign Affairs and the Conservative MP for Edinburgh Pentlands, declared that the SOE was a secret wartime organisation, whose activities must, in the public interest, remain secret. For this reason, he said, the organisation's files could not be made available to the public, and that a limited amount of information that was not secret could be provided in secret cases, and no distinction would be drawn between the records of those who had returned and those who had not.

It would appear that the only reason Dame Ward wanted sight of the SOE files was because she wanted to write a book about the organisation's wartime actions, although she did promise to submit the manuscript of her book to the Foreign Office for scrutiny and agreement before having it published. Her pleas fell on deaf ears.

On hearing the refusal by the Foreign Office to release the wartime files held on the SOE, Mr Lewis entered the fray by asking if the Minister was aware that he, Mr Lewis, had previously asked a number of questions concerning the SOE's conduct and actions in the Netherlands? He also wanted to know if Lord Hope had read the excellent book entitled *London Calling North Pole* by Lieutenant Colonel Giskes, stating that if he had, he would no doubt be ashamed at what had happened under this department's Special Operations Executive.

Lieutenant Colonel John Kyme Cordeaux, the Conservative MP for Nottingham Central was the next to enter the debate when he asked Lord Hope if he was aware that a number of amateur authors had published books about their wartime experiences concerning the secret services? He further asked whether Lord Hope would try to prevent other such publications from being printed by preventing access to the few remaining files that existed in relation to the work carried out and the methods used by the SOE and, if necessary, invoke the Official Secrets Act for the purpose.

It was abundantly clear from the exchange that no matter what was said, the Foreign Office was not willing to release files or any other related documents into the public domain concerning the SOE's wartime activities.

On Monday, 15 December 1958, Dame Irene Ward once again asked a question regarding the SOE. Also involved in the debate were Mr John Profumo, the Conservative MP for Stratford-upon-Avon, and Lieutenant Colonel John Kyme Cordeaux. The question asked was very similar to the one Dame Irene had put forward on 22 February

1956, when she enquired whether the Secretary of State for Foreign Affairs would make arrangements for information contained in the SOE's files to be made available to those who were interested.

In response, Mr Profumo said that for security reasons, it was not possible to allow members of the public to have direct access to the SOE's files, but that arrangements would be made by the Foreign Office to assign a former officer with wartime experience of the SOE to advise and assist inquirers with questions regarding the release of information concerning the organisation. In this instance, it would seem 'inquirers' meant anybody other than members of the general public.

This was certainly a very different response from the Foreign Office to the one it had given in February 1956. Lieutenant Colonel Cordeaux was of the same opinion as he had previously been, and he certainly did not hold back from making his opinion on the matter absolutely clear, aiming his comments directly at Mr Profumo, and wanting to know if he agreed that the suggestions made by Dame Irene had gone too far, and that enough damage had already been caused to Britain's Security Services by the publications that had already been allowed to come to print. Cordeaux wanted assurances from Mr Profumo that no more access would be allowed to SOE-related files to prevent their techniques and practices from being made available for public consumption.

Mr Profumo acknowledged that certain SOE operations had been subjected to criticism on a number of occasions, much of which had been damaging and irresponsible. Dame Irene then asked Mr Profumo if he would explain to Lieutenant Colonel Cordeaux that this new suggestion had in fact originated from the Foreign Office and thanked him for trying to find some way of ensuring that wild statements and rumours concerning the SOE were not spread all over the world without some distinction between what should properly be disclosed and what should not.

Mr Profumo, apparently happy that he had managed to sate Dame Irene's notorious, and potentially volatile persona, finished the debate by stating that he was grateful to have been able to help, but would prefer not to get between her and Lieutenant Colonel Cordeaux in the future.

On Monday, 2 May 1966 Dame Irene once again asked a question of the Secretary of State for Foreign Affairs during a sitting of the House of Commons about plans to write an official history of SOE operations in each European country, following the recent publication of one about France, and when he proposed to authorise the commencement of a book on operations in other countries.

Mrs Eirene White, the Parliamentary Under Secretary of State, and the Conservative MP for Flintshire East, responded on behalf of the Secretary of State by informing Dame Irene that there were no immediate plans to publish any histories of the SOE's activities in other countries.

Dame Irene, clearly not satisfied with what she had been told, continued to push the point, and for whatever reason did not appear to want to accept the answer she had been given, going as far as to suggest that it would be a good moment to start a history of the resistance in Norway, which had been particularly helpful to Britain during the war.

No explanation was provided by Mrs White as to why a history of the SOE's activities in France during the war had been published, but it was not deemed suitable to do the same for their involvement in other German-occupied countries.

It is quite amazing that twenty years after the SOE was formally disbanded, questions were still being raised about its activities in Parliament. Yet despite the fact the SOE was involved in numerous theatres of war between 1940 and 1945, it appears there has always been a reticence to talk about Operation North Pole and the agents who were dropped into the German-occupied the Netherlands between 1942 and 1943.

CHAPTER TWELVE

Post-War Press Articles About Operation North Pole

Stories about Operation North Pole only started appearing in the British Press as a direct result of the publication of the 1953 book by Hermann Giskes, *London Calling North Pole*. If it was not for this, the story may have never been revealed and would otherwise have remained a secret for many more years. Perhaps it would never have come to light and simply remained a secret of those dark and often depressing years?

The first fully comprehensive and detailed post war article about Operation North Pole appeared in the *Belfast Telegraph* newspaper dated Friday, 27 February 1953, under the headline, 'Story of war-time spying that makes uneasy reading'. This was a story that was not only published in a country still recovering from the war, even though it had ended some eight years previously. Indeed, it would be many more years before the entire world fully recovered from the personal loss and sacrifice people had endured.

The story highlighted to the British public that they did not know everything that had taken place during the war, and the shock that came with discovering the very existence of Operation North Pole had nothing to do with a feeling of betrayal, because there was none, but was more to do with a feeling of having been let down by the British authorities.

The story in the *Belfast Telegraph* told the public how British military intelligence had spent two years dropping SOE agents into the Netherlands, not knowing that they were being arrested immediately upon landing, and that later many of them were murdered in German-run concentration camps.

They were told how the German Abwehr had sent messages to British military intelligence in London by using the radio sets of captured British agents, their intention being to make the British authorities in London believe that their agents had arrived safely, were operational and carrying out their respective missions.

Not only were the agents later killed following their arrests, but as a result of these operations, a number of the aircraft used to deliver the agents to the drop off points were attacked, shot down and their crews killed.

For Hermann Giskes it became a massive juggling operation of information, which required him to continually supply London with updates from each of the captured radio sets, which was not always easy without giving the game away.

Giskes himself had no regrets about the work he had done and the results it had achieved, but he was sorry for the captured British agents whom he had promised to protect and safeguard. He had been promised, formally and in writing, by the German High Command that the captured agents would not be physically harmed, yet by the end of the war nearly all of those who had been captured were dead; murdered at the hands of their German captors. It was because of the shame and bitterness he felt as a result of this betrayal which had resulted in him writing his story.

Ten months later, and after Giskes' book had been thoroughly digested by historians, politicians, maybe even members of the British Secret Service, an article appeared in the *People* newspaper dated Sunday, 22 November 1953, under the heading of 'Spies gave us vital news – We gaoled 'em!'

The article was far from complimentary of the British Intelligence Service, speaking of how two agents had managed to escape from their captivity in Germany and make their way back to England with vital information about how all the agents who had been sent out to the Netherlands had been captured by the Germans, and that their radio sets had been used to send false messages.

The article went on to explain that rather than be met with gratitude and awards, they were not believed and instead were thrown into prison, alongside murderers, rapists, and the very worst of the criminal fraternity. It was only after months of interrogation and detention that they were finally believed and released, and only then because their stories were confirmed by reports by other agents of a similar nature.

The two agents Pieter Dourlein and Johan Ubbink, had both been dropped into the Netherlands as part of Operation North Pole, been captured by the Germans, held in custody, and then escaped. Their journey back to England had taken five months and seen them travel through Switzerland, France, Spain and Gibraltar.

Neither man could understand why British Intelligence had never realised that the German Abwehr had control of their radio, or the sets of other agents. It was a mystery even they did not understand.

Despite attempts by the newspaper to get some kind of response from the Foreign Office, all they received was, 'We have no comment to make'.

Part of the problem had arisen because of those who worked for MI6. Most if not all of those employed by the agency at the outbreak of the Second World War had been recruited from either Cambridge or Oxford universities by some of the tutors who worked there. It would be fair to say, therefore, that those who worked for MI6 not only came from the very top of British society but were very well-educated individuals who were seen as ideal candidates for the secret service. Academically, they were second to none. In comparison, those who worked for the SOE might not have been so highly educated, but they were street wise, practical and could think on their feet. It could be said that those at MI6 saw themselves as the more important partner of the two agencies; well-off individuals who came from well-known families within society. So, when two members of the SOE dared to raise questions about how poorly they were conducting themselves, it would not have gone down well with the 'old school tie chaps' from MI6.

As recently as 1993, articles about Operation North Pole were still appearing in the pages of British newspapers. The *Aberdeen*

Press and Journal dated Friday, 25 June of that year, included the headline, 'A Cover-up over the Secret War'.

The article began by explaining that the previous year, reports and documentation connected to Operation North Pole, and referring to Germanys penetration of the SOE's Dutch section, had been declassified and then inexplicably destroyed as recently as January 1992. This had in turn led in turn to allegations of a Whitehall cover up of its wartime failings.

The same article included information that the decision to 'destroy' this important documentation must have come from the very top of British government, as the person who signed for their release at the Public Record office at Kew was an unnamed official of Prime Minister John Major's office in Downing Street.

There was no secret of the fact that the SOE and British military intelligence did not get on with each other, to such a degree that the wartime Prime Minister Winston Churchill had given serious consideration to appointing a High Court Judge to act as an intermediate between the two agencies. Lord Selbourne, who in April 1942 had been Minister for Economic Warfare, had warned Churchill that the on-going discourse between the agencies was potentially dangerous. What, if anything, he did with that information is unclear.

It is absolutely staggering to read from this article that somebody, apparently in high office, took the decision to destroy such historical and important documents. The question remains, however, who made that decision, why, and who actually carried out the destruction? It would appear that it was done to protect the professional reputation of an individual, or individuals. Possibly with the knowledge that the documents in question were soon be made available for public consumption. Those responsible for this selfish act of wanton destruction should at least come forward and explain why they did what they did.

Conclusion

Is there a definitive answer as to what Operation North Pole was truly all about? Did Germany fool Britain between 1942 and 1944 or was it the other way around? Sadly, we will never know for sure, mainly because soon after the SOE was disbanded, nearly all its records were burnt in a mysterious fire in 1946.

It is true that Huub Lauwers was arrested by the Gestapo in March 1942 and was made to transmit messages back to London to cover up the fact that he had been captured. Despite making this clear in his messages to his handlers in London by altering his cypher accordingly, the British continued to send more and more agents across the English Channel, who were then immediately arrested after landing in the Netherlands.

It is incomprehensible to believe that the highly trained and dedicated individuals who were in place to receive the agents' messages in London missed the coded signals included in messages by Huub Lauwers. If this is true, then there are only two conceivable conclusions that can be drawn. The first is that the British authorities ignored Lauwers' warnings and carried on sending more and more agents and supplies into the Netherlands to make the Germans believe they had been successful, when the reality was that the British had double-bluffed the Germans, having deemed the Dutch agents to be expendable, so as to keep secret the fact that they knew their operation had been compromised and did not want the Germans to know it. The other possibility was that SOE headquarters in London had already been infiltrated by a high-ranking German spy, and it was he who had covered up the fact that Lauwers' messages contained notifications that he was sending them under duress.

It was as a direct result of Lauwers' messages that more and more SOE agents continued to be sent to the Netherlands, all of whom were captured and many of whom subsequently met their deaths in German concentration camps.

The unanswered question is why were all the inaccuracies and obvious mistakes that were included in a number of the messages sent back to London not recognised? It just does not make sense. The agents in the field did exactly what they had been taught to do during their training. They followed SOE policy and procedures, which catered for such eventualities, yet the mistakes and errors were not recognised, and more and more agents were dropped into the Netherlands, resulting in nearly all of them losing their lives. The truth is that all these years later, we are extremely unlikely to ever discover the truth behind why Operation North Pole continued for as long as it did.

List of Murdered Operation North Pole Agents at Mauthausen

A number of SOE agents were murdered in different countries throughout occupied Europe during the Second World War. Sometimes the exact location of a particular murder was not known with any degree of certainty, and the only available information provided is the agent's last known whereabouts, such as the camp at Rawicz.

The following names are those of captured British and Dutch agents who were executed at Mauthausen on 6 and 7 September 1944. A plaque outside the camp includes the following inscription (in German), about those who were murdered there:

40 Dutch and 7 British Special Agents who had been dropped over German occupied territory, on a special mission with great danger to their own lives, were cruelly put to death in this camp by the Nazis. Their bodies were burned in the camp crematorium.

Alblas, A H

Arendse, P A

Beukema toe Water, K W A

Boogaart, P C

Braggaar, C C

Buizer, J J C

Clement, G

Andringa, L TH C

Baatsen, A A

Bloome, M

van de Bor, K

de Brey, O W

Bukkens, J

Dane, J C

Drooglfevfr Fortuijn, C
De Haas, J H M
Hofstede, J
Jambroes, G L
Jongelie, R CH
Klooss, B
De Kruijff, A J
Mink, A B
Niermeijer, W J
Van Os, G
Punt, L M
Ras, G H G
Sebes, H
Taconis, TH
Wegner, A J
van der Wilden, W
Young, J C

Emmer, J
van Hemert, G J
van Hulsteijn, C E
Jones, S C
Kamphorst, P
Koolstra, M
Ter Laak, J H A M
Newman, I
Norman, G
Pals, M
Radema, E
Ruseler, G L
Steeksma, H R
van Uytvanck, I
van der Wilden, P
Wilkinson, F

Index